ATROPOS PRESS
new york • dresden

For Holly Marie Karibo.

Deleuze and the Sign

Christopher M. Drohan

Think Media EGS Series is supported by the European Graduate School

ATROPOS PRESS
New York • Dresden

US: 151 First Avenue # 14, New York, N.Y. 10003
Germany: Mockritzer Str. 6, D-01219 Dresden

cover design: Hannes Charen

ISBN 978-0-9819972-0-9

Preface

The following book aims to introduce scholars into the semiotics of Gilles Deleuze. In order to do so, we have had to extract and finish many of Deleuze's implicit arguments from often fragmentary and vague remarks. In the context of the rest of his works, readers can usually supplement the details that complete these arguments. However, for first time readers, or for those unfamiliar with the thousands (!) of sources he appeals to, these leaps can create a crippling vertigo that makes one want to give up reading in sheer aggravation. Obscure to the point of being entirely poetic at times, his books are certainly not 'easy reads.' And despite tackling many of the important concepts and traditions of so called 'analytical' and 'linguistic' philosophy, Deleuze's cryptic and often vague style of writing is enough to dissuade lovers of this philosophic bent from ever coming near his works.

His first major semiotic work, *Proust and Signs,* is no exception. As one of his earlier books, it contains a good number of half-finished concepts and ideas that only a comprehensive reading of his whole life's work could clarify. Nonetheless, Deleuze is a meticulous writer. Reading him, one is amazed at how consistent his entire ontology is, and how a seemingly haphazard idea is actually a part of an intricate and flawless logic underpinning his life's work. From *Proust and Signs* to his later texts, there is little that changed in his overall concept of the sign. What does change, however, is the terminology he uses to describe the various states and relations of signs, as well as the extent to which he's willing to push their underlying concepts towards even more astounding implications. Throughout, Deleuze notoriously uses synonyms of key terms and concepts, apparently at random. However, in the greater context of all his work these have each been chosen for particular reasons, usually to help make further sense of a complex idea. Apparent slips of the tongue are actually carefully chosen words, meant to have an overall effect on the reader that involuntarily initiates them into his worlds.

It is with this ambiguity in mind that this introduction to Deleuze's concept and theory of the sign has been created. It is our intention to help bridge the gap between so called 'continental' and 'analytical' treatments of the sign, at least in part, so that Deleuze's contribution to the philosophy of the sign can be seen as the legitimate and revolutionary work that it is.

Accordingly, throughout this book we continually show where Deleuze's concepts fit into modern semiotic discourse, and how he breaks with this tradition in order to establish his own unique semiotic ideas. At the same time, we not only synthesize his arguments, but also complete and extend his concepts so as to remove much of the ambiguity surrounding them. Where appropriate, we also attempt to reconcile Deleuze's work with that of other philosophers, showing how these works intersect and inform his own.

Thus, with patience and the utmost charity, we now wander into Deleuze's worlds, not only to understand them, but also to extend them beyond their own boundaries, to the point at which these worlds are created, which is to say the point through which understanding is even possible.

Chapter I

The Search for Strange Worlds: Deleuzian Semiotics and Proust

When one reads, one likes to be transported into a new world.

- Marcel Proust[1]

In his first major semiotic work, *Proust and Signs*, Deleuze not only ignores the whole field of semiotics, but the entire history of the philosophy of the sign. In a bold affront to both, he instead uses Proust's masterwork *In Search of Lost Time* as if it were some authority on signs and their concept. Nothing short of scandalous, Deleuze wrestles the sign away from analytic scholarship towards an existential theory that is consistent with his material realism.

Now, the semiotician knows that literature is full of signs. Saussure himself, the accredited founder of the discipline, called language "a system of signs expressing ideas and hence comparable to writing" (Saussure 2005: 15). This concept, inherited from a long philosophic trend, idealizes the sign as a linguistic phenomenon and places the sign's truth within linguistic structure.[2]

Deleuze, on the other hand, approaches this history and discipline from a different angle. For him, the work of literature abounds in signs. Therefore, by analyzing a text we can trace the emergence of those signs, both within the worlds of that book

---

[1] Proust VI: 280.
[2] Thomas Sebeok offers a convenient summary in *Signs: An Introduction to Semiotics* (Sebeok 2001: 4-11).

and before the readers of them. The question of the sign has been reversed: if signs are systems comparable to writing, literature will be full of systems of signs ripe for investigation. Different texts will use different sign systems or, as Deleuze will later call them, different "regimes" of signs, complete with their own rules and limitations.[3]

Proust is rich material for such a study. The *Search* overflows with signs and sign systems, the manifestation of which is painstakingly detailed in the narrator's desperate attempts to uncover the truth of his past. Reading Proust, one must question not only what the narrator is searching for, but why he is searching in the first place. For if we take this search as seriously as Proust does, we see that "the *Search* is not simply an effort of recall, an exploration of memory: search, *recherche*, is to be taken in the strong sense of the term, as we say "the search for truth"" (Deleuze 1972: 3).

It is precisely because we do not know the 'truth' of a sign that it strikes us existentially as being more than just an object that we understand, but as something that we must investigate and spend time with in order to unravel its meaning. To get to the 'truth' of a sign and to know it, we must 'apprentice' to that sign. We must ponder its relation to the world and to other signs. In fact, without signs we would not be able to learn at all:

---

[3] Later, in *A Thousand Plateaus*, Deleuze will also discover four regimes of signs that represent four socio-political regimes that result when the state itself controls its signs differently, namely: the primitive state and pre-signifying semiotic, where signs use up their names and significations as soon as they are found; the despotic state and signifying regime, where all signs must correspond to explicit meanings that are enforced by law in the state that desires to signify everything and have nothing outside its domain; the counter-signifying semiotic and nomadic war machine, which is always against the despotic state, mixing empires and regimes of signs, and destroying or hybridizing them; and the post-signifying regime, where everything is subject to its own proceeding, judged in a virtual tyrannical model. The four different types of signs in Proust become these four different types of semiotics and politics. For instance, the worldly sign is like its own pre-signifying regime; the signs of love are the beginning of signification and the signifying regime; the sensuous signs all function in a mixed and counter-signifying semiotic; while the signs of art each represent a virtual and infinite world which becomes so many significant and subjective worlds and proceedings (*TP*, pp.111-35). See chapter III for more.

Learning is essentially concerned with *signs*. Signs are the object of a temporal apprenticeship, not of an abstract knowledge. To learn is first of all to consider a substance, an object, a being as if they emitted signs to be deciphered, interpreted. There is no apprentice who is not "the Egyptologist" of something. One becomes a carpenter only by becoming sensitive to the signs of wood, a physician by becoming sensitive to the signs of disease. Vocation is always predestination with regard to signs. Everything which teaches us something emits signs, every act of learning is an interpretation of signs or hieroglyphs. Proust's work is based not on the exposition of memory, but on the apprenticeship to signs (4).

Already, with these notions of the sign as a 'search' and learning as an 'interpretation of signs', Deleuze has begun wrestling the sign away from analytic definitions of its phenomenon, towards a pragmatic and existential probing of its nature. Instead of asking *what* a sign is, he asks *how* it is that we discover, interpret, and use signs in the first place.

On the one hand, his concepts fit the work done by Peirce (later taken up by Eco and Sebeok, among many others). It was Peirce that declared, "a sign is something by knowing which we know something more," and that "all reasoning is an interpretation of signs of some kind" (Peirce: 332). Deleuze agrees with these ideas, and gladly declares that signs lead us to new knowledge. However he surpasses these notions by questioning the process of knowledge itself that the sign inaugurates. If knowing the sign brings more knowledge, and this is a process of 'learning,' what does the process of 'learning' the sign entail? First and foremost, Deleuze asserts that there must be an interpretation of those signs. To know the sign, one must interpret them. In other words, they must *search* for that knowledge. There is a radical shift taking place here. Deleuze is wrestling the sign away from a strictly analytic definition of the sign, towards a pragmatic and existential probing of its nature. More than abstractly saying what a sign is equivalent to (i.e. knowledge, knowing, and knowing more), or what a sign is (i.e. some knowledge in excess of the sign), Deleuze pushes the sign towards questions of praxis. Towards this end, he allies himself with existentialists like Heidegger:

> We shall never learn what "is called" swimming, for example,
> or what it "calls for," by reading a treatise on swimming. Only
> the leap into the river tells us what is called swimming. The
> question "What is called thinking?" can never be answered by
> proposing a definition of the concept *thinking*, and then
> diligently explaining what is contained in that definition. In
> what follows, we shall not thing *about* what thinking is. We
> remain outside that mere reflection which makes thinking its
> object (Heidegger: 21).

The focus turns away from 'what' a sign is, towards 'how' it is
that we discover and interpret signs in the first place. Above and
beyond the sign's definition, we need to trace its emergence and
the entire process that leads from its existence to a rudimentary
knowledge of its place in the world. By focusing on this search,
Deleuze is recognizing that the question of the sign is much
broader than it has usually been treated in the history of
philosophy and semiotics. Understanding the concept of the sign
is inseparable from understanding how it exists before us and
how that existence comes to pass. *Proust and Signs* is Deleuze's
first attempt at tracing these movements, and the book represents
his first articulation of the fundamental arguments and positions
that dominate all his writings on the sign.

   He begins this work by pointing out that a sign is a sign
on account of our engagement with it. The sign *affects* us. In its
presence we are filled with feelings that set it apart from other
objects and which make us aware that there is much more to it
than its mere presence at hand. Deleuze observes that a sign can
fill us with "nervous exaltation" (Deleuze 1972: 7), "jealousy",
or the "joys" and "sufferings" of many different "sensuous
impressions" (11, 12). Its signing is constituted by this
existential grip on us that demands we overcome its mere
appearance in order to fully explore its relation, both to the
feeling it conjures within us, and to the other actions and
thoughts surrounding it.

   Think of the narrator of the *Search* with his "petite
madeleine" and tea. Upon tasting it, he declares that its
sensation:

had the effect, which love has, of filling me with a precious essence; or rather this essence was not in me, it *was* me. I had ceased now to feel mediocre, contingent, mortal. Whence could it have come to me, this all-powerful joy? I sensed that it was connected with the taste of the tea and the cake, but that it infinitely transcended those savours, [and] could not, indeed, be of the same nature. Where did it come from? What did it mean? How could I seize and apprehend it? (Proust I: 60).

Deleuze loved this example because everything is there: the sign overwhelming us, filling us with both joy and apprehension, compelling us to find its meaning. What does it mean? What is it that overwhelms us and surpasses this cake, this taste, this joy?:

I put down the cup and examine my own mind. It alone can discover the truth. But how? What an abyss of uncertainty, whenever the mind feels overtaken by itself; when it, the seeker, is at the same time the dark region through which it must go seeking and where all its equipment will avail it nothing. See? More than that: create. It is face to face with something which does not yet exist, which it alone can make actual, which it alone can bring into the light of day (Proust I: 61).

The narrator must 'seek' out the answers to these questions, not so much to find them, but to 'create' their meaning. Meanwhile, the sign is revealed as the production of meaning and of the various incarnations of an invisible essence assaulting us.

The first thing we can say *a posteriori* of the sign is that even though it emerges in relation to what we already know, it assails us because it has no place in that knowledge. Otherwise it would not *sign* to us, but would be understood immediately. Instead, it brutally exists before us as a recognizable but amorphous material, but also as a feeling that drives us beyond that material, motivating us to grasp its significance.

In the presence of a sign, though, the question remains: to what world, if not our own, does this sign belong? If the sign immediately has no place in our understanding and in the world we know, it necessarily represents *another* world with which we are not familiar. But upon its arrival, we are blocked from this foreign world of the sign. The sign seems caught between worlds, struggling to find expression in our understanding, but remaining attached to some other. It expresses some truth about both, but in a vague relation that needs to be exposed. Consequently, every sign inaugurates a search that may propel us into a new world, one with which we are, prior to the apprenticeship, unacquainted:

> The *Search* is presented as the exploration of different worlds of signs which are organized in circles and intersect at certain points, for the signs are specific and constitute the substance of one world or another (5).

From this perspective, the *Search* can be seen as an exploration of the different worlds of the narrator's past (e.g. the world of the Verdurins, Swann's world, the world of the Méséglise Way versus that of the Guermantes Way, or the worlds of Combray, Balbec, Doncières, etc.). As he follows their signs, the narrator builds these worlds in his own mind, blending them in and out of each other in ever increasing complexity. The narrator's hypermnesia immediately transforms him into a kind of astronaut, deep-sea diver, or spelunker of different worlds.[4]

Now, a world is a world because it has some degree of consistency, that is to say, some coherence in the meanings of its signs. If worlds are organized 'in circles,' it is because of the different codes of meaning between them. We must keep in mind that what a sign means in one world is not what it means in another; and it is the consistency of these distinct meanings that keeps these worlds apart, allowing them to function in different ways:

> The worlds are unified by the formation of sign systems, emitted by persons, objects, substances; we discover no truth, we learn nothing except by deciphering and interpreting. But the plurality of worlds is such that these signs are not of the same kind, do not have the same way of appearing, do not allow themselves to be deciphered in the same manner, do not have an identical relation with their meaning. The hypothesis that the signs form both the unity and the plurality of the *Search* must be verified by considering the worlds in which the hero participates directly (5).

---

[4] On the importance of amnesia and hypermnesia see Deleuze's *Negotiations* (138).

Epistemologically, a world remains a closed 'circle' or 'system' which preserves its space only by sustaining its individual codes and series of meanings. Signs and objects that do not adhere to these codes must be excluded, or else the circle can be opened and become part of another world. For example, think of how the 'little clan' of the Verdurins is defined by what the narrator can only call the "tacit" "Creed" of Mme. Verdurin and her husband (Proust I: 265). But Swann's strange codes do not always fit in there, as his worldly mannerisms, which have been assembled from other influential circles of acquaintance, threaten Mme. Verdurin. She begins to distrust him the moment she realizes his popularity and his sphere of influence, which link him to worlds larger than her own (Proust I: 307).[5] Jealous, she breaks ties with Swann before he can sweep away any member of her clan into these other worlds.[6]

It is only by deciphering the codes and relations of a sign that we begin to understand its systems of meaning (that is, its worlds and their plurality), and thus begin to see its grander significance. But we have not as yet reached the truth of the sign, for the truth of the sign exceeds its significance, both in the amorphous material of the sign, as well as in the insignificant search preceding and positing its meaning. The sign is more than its worlds and its concrete impressions: it is a "*precious essence*" (Proust I: 60),[7] which not only solicits materials, but also conducts their meaningful relations to each other. Meanwhile, this essence somehow also manages to evade these concrete instantiations, allowing it to continue repeating its invisible production of these differences.

---

[5] Or, in contrast, consider Saint-Loup's little circle at Balbec to which the narrator gains entrance by repeating all the same styles and codes of behavior, but in which Bloch fails because he has not mastered the rules (Proust II: 374-75).

[6] In contrast, consider Saint-Loup's little circle at Balbec, which the narrator gains entrance to by repeating all the same styles and codes of behavior, but which Bloch fails in because he has not mastered the rules (Proust II: 308-359).

[7] These are Proust's words, but Deleuze takes the term for his own and launches into a complete philosophical treatment of them, both in *Proust and Signs* and in all his subsequent works (39-51). See in particular *Expressionism and Philosophy: Spinoza* (Deleuze 1992: 191-200).

Proust's hero discovers firsthand how signs evade their concrete meanings and how they repeatedly reveal new 'truths' as they are pursued. While circulating among the upper echelons of French society, and in the subjective worlds of his memories, the narrator discovers signs that repeat from one world to the next. With every leap, though, the meaning of any particular sign can either change or become infinitely more complex. What he thinks he knows in one circle of acquaintances fails in another, and in the array of different circles the meaning of every sign becomes layered.[8] Consider the 'petite madeleine' again: its sign means the object of the cake, but also elicits the memory of aunt Léonie and Sunday mornings in Combray, and:

> the old grey house upon the street [...] the garden which had been built out behind it [...] and with the house the town, from morning to night and in all weathers, the Square where I used to be sent before lunch, the streets along which I used to run errands, the country roads we took when it was fine (Proust I: 64).

So many different meanings are at play here, all charging towards their own worlds, "moved as if by magic" (Proust VI: 255). Accordingly, in Proust, Deleuze uncovers four basic kinds of signs which in turn correspond to four different kinds of worlds. These signs differ in kind from each other primarily because of our existential disposition towards them and the extent to which we are willing to tarry in their search.

The sign always already materializes within an entire existential framework. Its meaning is composed both within what we already know, as well as in the context of our desire to know it; this is the insignificant intensity we bear towards it. Insignificant, because existentially the sign agitates us, but the

---

[8] For instance, in vol. I alone, the narrator explicitly declares the existence of various worlds: the inner "world" of the narrator's bedroom (7), "the unknown world" of women (119), the two "planes" of the narrator's image of Mme. de Guermantes and her actual presence (247-49), the little phrase by Vinteuil which was "another world" for Swann (308), and the world of emotions vs the "world of colours" induced in the narrator by Gilberte (591). But every episode and scene within the work constitutes its own world, made up of its own objects and signs: Combray, Mme. de Villeparisis's house, Swann's Way, the Guermantes Way, the Verdurins' Circle, the Marquise de Saint-Euverte's, the Champs-Elysées, the Bois de Boulogne, the Méséglise Way, Balbec, etc.

meaning of that agitation is unspecified until we have apprenticed with it. Instead, our search expresses a plethora of ways that we can relate to it and thus a simultaneous multiplicity of meanings. On a strictly material level, it is not that the sign perpetually changes, but instead that in our search we change our relation to that sign, and thus constantly alter both its significant meaning and its insignificant desire.

Of this multiplicity, the most basic expression of meaning occurs in what Deleuze calls the "worldly sign". Let us trace its movement. We stumble upon a sign. This sign, in turn, is a sign because it is coupled with a feeling that obliges us to search for its meaning. It leaps out at us from materiality and demands that we apprentice with it until we can discover its 'truth'. But what is it that is leaping out at us? What is a 'worldly sign'?:

> The worldly sign appears as the replacement of an action or thought. It stands for action and for thought. It is therefore a sign which does not refer to something else, to a transcendent signification or to an ideal content, but which has usurped the supposed value of its meaning. This is why worldliness, judged from the viewpoint of actions, appears to be disappointing and cruel; and from the viewpoint of thought, it appears stupid. One does not think and one does not act, but one makes signs (Deleuze 1972: 6).

To begin with, the sign is still somewhat attached to the significant action or thought from which it sprung. However, by 'replacing' this action or thought, Deleuze means that the sign refuses this signification, instead signifying something else. Where a sign replaces a thought, it 'appears stupid' because it no longer shares the meaning of the thought it replaces. It is meaningless and nonsensical. Where a sign replaces an action, it 'appears to be disappointing and cruel' because it has no connection to the course of actions hitherto. It is clumsy or awkward, the sign of an action with no bearing.

Although materially identical to them, the sign cannot be declared a specific action or thought because it does not yet have significance. It is entirely meaningless, only becoming an action or thought after it relates to other materials. There is no transcendent signifier at work, no ideal correspondence of the sign to a preordained set of materials; there is only a coincidence of material relations which somehow express each other so as to become actions and thoughts.

Deleuze's emphasis on the amorphousness of the sign, and its ability to depose meaningful actions and thoughts, discloses his implicit concept of meaning: namely that a meaning is forged when one concrete material correlates to another. The 'search' is this process, wherein materiality spontaneously creates these correlative bonds, these simple codes of meaning.

First, the sign correlates immediately to its own material, while our affection expresses itself in that material. And that is when "the sign's meaning appears, yielding to us the concealed object" (11-12). When the amorphous feeling of a sign and the amorphous material eliciting that feeling correlate, both 'meaning' and the 'object' are produced. They mutually articulate each other, creating a meaning that is entirely redundant. Deleuze calls this redundancy "*objectivism*" (26). Objectivism is not to be confused with 'objectivity', which has its own concept and history in philosophy. Nor is it an obscure reference to Ayn Rand.[9] No, Deleuze's concept is uniquely his own, and has a very particular sense. In Deleuze's objectivism, we "attribute to the object the signs it bears" and "we think that the "object" itself has the secret of the signs it emits" (26-27). For instance, the narrator realizes that the madeleine and tea are the object of the sign he receives, but this tells him nothing, and he devours the cake knowing there is something more there (i.e. the memories haunting him) (Proust I: 64).

To succumb to objectivism and to interpret the sign only in terms of its own object does not bring us any new knowledge about the sign. Rather, it is more like a habitual association or the natural tendency to associate the sign with what is closest to hand.[10] At most, it gives us a mere image of

---

[9] Rand developed both an ethical and epistemological theory called "Objectivism" throughout her writings. Specifically, see her *Introduction to Objectivist Epistemology*.
[10] One cannot help but see a connection between Deleuze's account of objectivism and Hume's "association of ideas" in *A Treatise of Human Nature*. The "constant conjunction of resembling perceptions" are the "causes of our ideas", the meaning of which are extended and compounded in the faculties of

the sign, but this is an image without significance, a mere correlation of perceptions.

In contrast, if we are to know this sign's *significance*, we must surpass this superficial meaning and explore the sign's relation to *other* signs and objects. Deleuze says:

> Each sign has two halves: it *designates* an object, it *signifies* something different. The objective side is the side of pleasure, of immediate delight and of practice. Taking this way, we have already sacrificed the "truth" side. We recognize things, but we never know them. What the sign signifies we identify with the person or object it designates. We miss our finest encounters, we avoid the imperatives which emanate from them: to the exploration of encounters we have preferred the facility of recognitions (Deleuze 1972: 26).

In objectivism, we 'designate' the sign by correlating its feeling to the particular object that existentially strikes us. This gives new meaning to both, for they are now understood in terms of each other and we are filled with the immediate pleasure of knowing the sign's reference. Coupled with the feeling of the sign, the object takes on a greater significance and the potential to reveal even more signs, objects and worlds. On this account, Deleuze calls them "worldly signs" (5-6), for they represent our passage into another world and our first contact with the unfamiliar essence that signifies so much more.

However, in light of the worldly sign's greater significance, its meaning-as-object quickly becomes nothing but a "disappointment". Let us consider, for example, all the narrator's disappointments: "Disappointment on first hearing Vinteuil, on first meeting Bergotte, on first seeing the Balbec church" or "[w]hen he sees, then comes to know Mme. de Guermantes" (32-33). The sign of them all, which could mean so much, attaches itself onto these base materials, these first impressions; but this does little to help us know them beyond this completely superficial meaning. Instead, the same existential compulsion that led us to associate the sign with its designated object now pushes us to understand that object in

_____

memory and imagination (Hume: 14-25). For more on the faculty of imagination and the meaning of signs, see Chapter V.

terms of others; and beyond the sign's designation, we begin looking for its significance, that is, its meaning relative to other meaningful objects and signs. Instead of an amorphous material signing to us, it is as if the entire object becomes a sign and we begin correlating it to other objects, learning more about its place in the world as we go.

We encounter a different type of sign at this point, a sign which allows us to extend its meaning. This other side of the sign is entirely subjective, for it emerges from within our feeling that the sign means more than its object and bears a personal significance above and beyond objective associations. Accordingly, Deleuze calls these the signs "of love", for, in Proust, these are best exemplified by those characters possessed by "love's signs" (7-9). The lover refuses to take their beloved's signs at face value, imagining all sorts of hidden worlds they could possibly signify. Consider the signs the narrator receives from Albertine: touches, glances, notes, all of which he interprets to mean some affection, but which he ultimately misreads (Proust V: 684). Or, the signs Swann receives from Odette: are these genuine signs of affection, or is she hiding a secret affair? The signs of love are open to interpretation, as if their truth resides in an unknown sphere:

> Love's signs are not like the signs of worldliness; they are not empty signs, standing for thought and action. They are deceptive signs which can be addressed to us only by concealing what they express: the origin of unknown worlds, of unknown actions and thoughts which give them a meaning. [...] The interpreter of love's signs is necessarily the interpreter of lies (Deleuze 1972: 9).

We are forever blocked from our beloved's inner worlds which they reveal to us as signs and objects whose exact meaning we do not know. Instead, we interpret them through our own understanding and give them a meaning that is entirely artificial and subjective, drawn from our own experience. Our search is confined to the objects it knows, linking them in all sorts of series of expression, trying frantically to get to the truth of them. But the more we search them, the more interpretations we reach.

Swann reels in conspiracies when he finds a letter from Odette to Forcheville:

> His jealousy, like an octopus which throws out a first, then a second, and finally a third tentacle, fastened itself firmly to that particular moment, five o'clock in the afternoon, then to another, then to another again [...], the perpetuation of a suffering that had come from without. (Proust I: 402-03).

The signs of love indicate hidden worlds which all come 'from without' so that they cannot be revealed by any object we know.

We encounter a third type of sign here, an inversion of the first two and their worlds. Insofar as the sign has meaning in an object or in a subjective series of objects, this meaning is achieved only by what it simultaneously excludes, namely the sign's relation to other objects and understandings. The sign still signifies these, only differently and in different series. The more we search this sign, the more we are led past its subjective meanings into its universality and its ability to express and signify infinite objects and worlds.

Deleuze calls them "sensuous qualities" or "sensuous signs" (Deleuze 1972: 39, 54). The feeling produced by the sign becomes perpetual, expressed in one object then another, one world then the next. It becomes a quality of them all, universally shared by them, but bearing different and even contradictory meanings in each. For instance, the narrator's love of the name Guermantes implies a range of ideas: the memory of the Guermantes Way, the social worlds of the Hôtel de Guermantes, the opera, Mme. de Villeparisis', not to mention Mme. de Guermantes' style of dress and different ways of conducting herself (Proust I: 188, 256-62).[11] The 'place-name' Guermantes is not just an object of a subjective infatuation, but the sign and quality of all these strange worlds.

These sensuous signs each allude to a much more profound essence at work, incarnated by their search and by all the meanings produced through them. Beneath them is a fourth kind of sign, a sign with the infinite potential to be taken up again and again and searched all over, producing endless

---

[11] However, it is not until vol. III that these worlds are firmly established and begin to take on a life different from what the narrator imagined in his youth.

concrete meanings without succumbing to any one of them. This fourth type of sign, this essence, is not so much a sign as much as it is the power of signing itself. Unlike sensuous signs or qualities, which always have a concrete sense, the essences are instead the immaterial forces that produce these concrete phenomena in the first place. Deleuze calls them "signs of art" (Deleuze 1972: 39), denoting their productive capacity which is ontological and which imparts signs, objects, significations and worlds all at once:

> What is the superiority of the signs of art over all the others? It is that the others are material. Material, first of all, by their emission: they are half sheathed in the object bearing them. Sensuous qualities, loved faces are still matter. (It is no accident that the significant sensuous qualities are above all odors and flavors: the most material of qualities.) *Only the signs of art are immaterial* [...], art gives us the true unity: unity of an immaterial sign and of an entirely spiritual meaning. The essence is precisely this unity of sign and meaning as it is revealed in the work of art (39-41).

Art becomes the object just as it becomes the qualities and meanings associated with that object. Yet, when we consider all of these material substantiations individually, we see that none of them captures the immaterial spirit of their creation. In contrast, when taken holistically, all of these materials vaguely outline a work of art that constantly exceeds its own dimensions, erupting in new impressions, signs, and insights at every moment.

Not coincidentally, Proust's anecdotes about art all allude to the explosive power of these essences. For example, the dramatic art of La Berma is more than a presentation on stage: it is the narrator's love and infatuation, her myth and charisma, the social circles at the opera, and the private worlds of the Guermantes. Or consider the musical art of Vinteuil, which symbolizes "another world" for Swann and still another for the narrator (Proust I: 308). Meanwhile, the paintings of Elstir display countless worlds that forever alter the way the narrator views Balbec (Proust II: 479). Regardless of its form or medium, art leads us to these radical transformations and creations which change our worlds and divulge an essence that surpasses all our understanding.

Accordingly, Deleuze conceives of all signs as ontologically being part of two different levels. On the one hand, the sign is concrete, distinctly perceived as some feeling, objectively articulated by some object and significantly related to other objects and multiple worlds. This concrete level is hierarchized epistemologically into its own levels of meaning: amorphous concrete materials and signs express each other to become meaningful objects; objects express each other to become significations; while significations express each other to create individual worlds, each with their own codes and "over-codes" that preserve them from each other (Deleuze & Guattari 1987: 8-9, 62).

On the other hand, and at another level, the sign is completely immaterial, amorphous, and virtual. In Proust's words, it is "real without being actual, ideal without being abstract" (Proust IV: 264). It is an essence which inheres within all the materials it expresses, but which is not signified completely by any one of them. It is "pure matter which is entirely distinct from the matter of the common things that we see and touch but of which [...] they too had seemed to me to be composed" (Proust IV: 270). This sign is rather searched *through* all of these 'common things' and expressed significantly *by* all of them simultaneously, so that its truth is multifarious, inter-subjective, multi-worldly, infinite, and utterly schizophrenic.

For Deleuze, the *Search* displays all these levels at once, but only as we relate to it, and only insofar as we are willing to search its signs ourselves and chase their essences. In light of Deleuze's account, we cannot help but read Proust differently. To begin with, we never read Proust, we search Proust. *In Search of Lost Time* is not so much a significant work of literature, but a sort of anti-literature, a collection of signs that explode into worlds. We search Proust at least four times: first as a collection of powerful signs and objects, bound by a literary essence that gathers signs capable of generating their own worlds and series. Rather than scenes and chapters in Proust, we find worlds which fold over one another and into one another in all directions. Second, as lovers of Proust, we should give him a paranoiac reading that strives to understand everything about his hidden worlds: how all the worlds relate literally and the signs that unite them; the references implied by the text and the historical context in which it was written; the structures and motifs of language that he uses to produce his effects, etc. In other words, we should undertake a scholastic reading of the master of literature and the rebel of its discipline. Third, we must give Proust a sensuous reading, allowing it to overwhelm our faculties until we see the signs and qualities of his worlds in our own. Only then can we embrace Proust and his worlds as techniques of living and responding to life: Cardiff as Combray or Toronto as Balbec.[12] Finally, we must produce through, and with, the essence of Proust. We must allow Proust to inspire us towards art, towards an infinite creation that is never our own, but neither is it his. Rather, it is something in-between, an altogether different essence which blossoms between them throughout our lives.

---

[12] This concept of art as a "life technique" is accredited to Schirmacher (Casey & Embree 1990: 5-39).

Chapter II

Towards an Existential Concept of the Sign: The Worldly Search

Signs grip us and impress upon us because we are not familiar with their meanings. In the absence of meaning, we conjure up all sorts of feelings and impressions, soliciting these in the attempt to give each sign some relation to our very being. Signs pique our curiosity, conjuring up feelings of excitement and playfulness, or even apprehension and fear. These emotions and impressions are the precursors of every sign's significant meaning, emerging amorphously between the sign and all the objects we know, captivating us so as to relate them to each other, and eventually articulating the sign in objective terms.

Only by giving our attention to the sign and searching it can we begin to see its wider relation to the world. In our apprenticeship towards the sign, we not only attempt to know the sign, but involuntarily, through that knowing, we discover more about the world itself. The sign is therefore a becoming, not only of its own meaning, but of the entire world in which we live. This is why Deleuze declares that all learning "is essentially concerned with *signs* (Deleuze 1972: 4)." It is signs that expose new relations in our world, and it is the search of signs that creates the most basic meanings through which we know the world.

Meanwhile, the world is filled with signs, which then take their place among the various meaningful things that we distinguish:

> The first world of the *Search* is the world of, precisely, worldliness. There is no milieu which emits and concentrates

> so many signs, in such reduced space, at so great a rate. It is
> true that these signs themselves are not homogeneous. At one
> and the same moment they are differentiated, not only
> according to classes but according to even more fundamental
> "families of mind". From one moment to the next, they evolve,
> crystallize, or give way to other signs (5-6).

Worldliness is the heterogeneity of all materials, and therefore
the origin of all signs. These worldly signs get compounded and
exchanged through the powers of worldliness into various
'families of mind'. By 'families of mind', Deleuze refers to the
various series of understandings that we make of worldliness.
Signs join these in order to gain different meanings and to help
us extend our overall knowledge of the world.

Ironically, the meaninglessness of the sign stems more
from an excess of meaning, than some sort of lack. Signs are
entirely positive in nature, signifying the overwhelming powers
of worldliness, which gives forth the sign in addition to its
plurality of associations. After all, this is what compels us to
search the sign: although we do not know where or to what the
sign belongs, existentially we feel that it is rife with potential,
associated not only to those feelings, but to everything else we
know. Rather painstakingly we must play with the sign,
following all its associations until its meaning is revealed in
some action or thought, or until its search is surrendered to
another one.

The very fact that Deleuze can judge the sign from the
viewpoint of actions or thoughts insinuates that the sign is itself
something like an action/thought. However Deleuze never
explicitly calls it such, precisely because he cannot. When he
says that one "does not think and one does not act, but one
makes signs", he implies that the sign comes from outside of the
various series of actions and thoughts, and although materially
identical to actions and thoughts, cannot be declared a specific
action/thought because it does not yet have a specific meaning
(6). The sign is entirely meaningless, and only becomes an
action/thought in relation to other actions and thoughts. Whereas
thinking and acting merely recycle known thoughts and actions,
the sign emerges between them as some other meaningless thing.
We recognize this affect and we are distinctly conscious of this

thing that emerges from the action/thought, but it has yet to take its place in the series of all actions or thoughts, wherein it would find meaning by allowing these to express it and give it overall relation to our worlds.

Understanding and meaning come subsequent to signs, after they have been formed into series with each other. Insofar as signs are associated with other impressions, they begin to correlate to these impressions in mutual expressions. The sign expresses its impressions as much as those impressions express it, such that all of them are bound in series with each other. It is at this point that we can speak of actions and thoughts, for the sign now relates to a particular set of materials, which give it explicit meaning.

As the search facilitates these meaningful correlations, it spontaneously reveals materiality's ability to create meaning itself. The search, therefore, existentially unites our world and all our understandings with materiality, if only briefly, towards the creation of new meanings and understandings. Signs, in turn, are the precursors of these openings and of the redistribution and extension of our knowledge. Fundamentally though, we are indebted to materiality, the powers of which supply the very signs and meanings that we consider.

Thus the search is none other than our ability to identify and distinguish actions/thoughts from actions/thoughts, uniting them in meaningful correlations. Were it not for signs, our universe would remain inert, undistinguished, and meaningless, for the search of them differentiates *materiality* into individual *materials*. Throughout this process, more signs may appear, such that a vicious circle repeats between signs and searches, despite the meaningful actions and thoughts they reveal. Accordingly, the search is resolved in meaning just as much as it is unresolved in the spontaneous emergence of new signs. It really all depends on materiality. Sometimes a meaning is found for a sign, and that is the end of the matter. However, there is nothing to say that something meaningful will not become a sign once more. The perpetual emergence of signs and searches forces us to constantly rearrange our understandings, rendering meaningful signs meaningless again.

That there are multiple series of these understandings implies an explicit difference in kind between a sign's 'meaning' and its 'understanding'. In Proust, a sign means different things depending on the series of understanding in which it is engaged (e.g. the madeleine, and its many senses). These series exclude each other by the limitations they put on their signs. Relative to each series, every sign is correlated to a different set of materials than any other series of understanding. Meanwhile, these codified sets of materials are what constitute the differences between one understanding of a sign and another. Therefore, the specific meaning of a sign is relative to its composite series of understanding, while series of understanding encompass multiple meanings, but only a particular and codified meaning for every sign they contain.

Let us reserve the term '*meaning*' for the most basic correlation of one material to another, regardless of whether it is in series with others (and understood) or not. The sign becomes meaningful the moment its impression correlates to another, so that the two share a mutual expression. Meaning is essentially 'binary' in that it requires at least two distinct materials paired to each other. In contrast, we shall reserve the term '*understanding*' for compound series of those basic meanings. We understand when basic meanings begin to correlate to each other, implicating an entire set of meanings, or a 'series' of understanding.

For the most part, Deleuze uses the term 'knowledge' synonymously with 'understanding' (26). To know is therefore to know something according to a series of understanding. In his later writings though, knowledge is distinguished from understanding as belonging more to those abstract series of understanding that encompass and organize multiple series of understandings together in broader relations. These relations are entirely abstract, in that they 'understand' understandings themselves. Knowledge, therefore, becomes a higher degree of intelligent organization, the point where understanding represents itself to itself. Just like meanings represent meanings so that they are understood, understandings represent understandings so that we can abstract them and separate them into various disciplines and domains of knowledge.

In *Proust and Signs*, Deleuze lays down the foundations of an intellectual hierarchy that is elemental to his entire semiotics. Basic meanings build themselves into series of understanding, which in turn unite and divide into worlds. All meanings, understandings, and worlds holistically constitute our 'knowledge' of the world, while our knowledge of the world ultimately depends on the extent to which we are willing to search materiality and our willingness to be open to new signs and new meanings from out of worldliness.

Aside from neglecting the argument for how it is that these worlds are composed (which is found much later in *Thousand Plateaus*),[13] Deleuze also neglects to explain our compulsion to search and our dissatisfaction with our own knowledge. Instead, these are both simply attributed to the sign and the effects it has upon us. Meanwhile, the precise relation between the sign and our desire to search is elaborated no further than mere insinuation. At the same time, Deleuze insists that our ability to understand and our desire for more knowledge come to us entirely from the level of materiality, yet he does not delve into how this level is the ontological source of both our desire and our ability to learn.

Furthermore, Deleuze fails to develop another important conclusion of this argument, namely that it is a meaningless materiality that ontologically produces real meaning. The various arguments for this position are not fully developed until he writes *Logic of Sense*, years later. Suffice to say, understanding and meaning come entirely from the meaningless chaos of materiality. Materiality supplies both the signs (meaningless impressions) and the correlations of them that allow for the meanings that we understand.

Thirdly, Deleuze never really explains what a sign is generally, neither in *Proust and Signs*, nor in any of his works. Fortunately, it is not hard to deduce. If actions/thoughts give way to signs, and those signs are meaningless until they correlate to other actions/thoughts, the sign is like a solitary impression or affect which is associated with others, without specifically correlating to any of them. *Signs are therefore*

---

[13] See the chapter, "10,000 B.C.: The Geology of Morals (Who Does the Earth Think It Is?)" (39-74).

infinitely meaningful impressions, which are simultaneously associated with all the other impressions and objects surrounding them. In searching signs, we surpass their infinite associations and give them specific correlations to other materials, at which point they become finite actions/thoughts. These actions/thoughts are then free to correlate to others, in series of understanding radiating out from the initial impressions of their signs. Together these series make up the worlds of signs, the extent of which depends on the overall relation of each sign to our entire knowledge, as well as the even greater context of its place in the world. Different times, spaces, desires, and prior knowledge will create different actions and thoughts through and with the same sign. *Therefore, no sign can claim to have a universal or 'ideal' meaning, namely because its meaning is relative to the signs, actions/thoughts, and worlds surrounding it*

Accordingly, there are different types of signs depending on the context in which a sign unfolds. In tracing his concept of the sign, Deleuze first takes stock of the different types of signs, so as to expose their common traits and how they become an infinite variety of materials and worlds. He begins with those found in the worlds of Proust, narrowing them down into four basic genera.

Throughout this taxonomy, Deleuze's analysis remains primarily existential, which means that his reduction neglects the *a priori* arguments for the existence of signs and their searches. These he will later borrow from Spinoza, from whom he will gather a more general material concept of the sign.[14] Nonetheless, in *Proust and Signs* he maintains that the different types of signs have much in common, and that they all share in a common essence and truth. Although the different types of signs and their relations introduce and sustain different worlds respectively, Deleuze holds that they are all still fundamentally part of the same material stratum. Thus, even in *Proust and Signs* Deleuze champions material realism, observing and asserting that all worlds share a common materiality.

Throughout *Proust and Signs,* Deleuze describes this worldliness in a variety of different ways. Moreover, we will see how he shows that worldliness is as much material and concrete

---

[14] See chapter V.

as it is immaterial and productive. For now though, Deleuze merely wants to draw a difference in terminology, referring to the material world in general as '*worldliness*' or '*the* world,' while the various material signs within it become part of their own singular '*world*' (i.e. '*a* world'). A world is characterized by its system of signs and semiotic relations, while the world is the material reality in which all these systems participate and are simultaneously connected:

> the world has no significant contents according to which we could systematize it, nor ideal significations according to which we could regulate and hierarchize it (Deleuze 1972: 143).

The world concurrently encompasses all systems, in addition to all those signs, materials, and material relations that are not systematized, but which exist along side systems, still relatively meaningless. The world is, therefore, simultaneously both the significant and insignificant materiality in and from which all things are wrought, which ontologically subsists before and within them all.

This infinite and chaotic materiality organizes itself into these various things, which in turn form relations with each other in order to constitute individual worlds. These individual worlds are entirely significant, abounding with their own chains of significations and meanings. But, in order to understand how this process of self-organization works, we need to trace the existential unfolding of the sign as it emerges for us in a particular world. In other words, we need to discover the threshold at which the most basic meanings are being created, for it is there that the sign is at work and there that we will find its concept.

Chapter III

The Four Types of Signs in Proust

A. The Worldly Signs
(Objective Signs)

Deleuze's hypothetical sign emerges from out of materiality, but in relation to some action or thought that it replaces. With this sign before us, "a kind of obligation is felt, the necessity of a mental effort: to seek the sign's meaning... Then, the sign's meaning appears, yielding to us the concealed object" (Deleuze 1972: 11-12). The sign's existential dimension demands that we give its impression meaning. But as the sign's impression emerges along side others and is associated with them, there is always the possibility of attributing it to one of these in a meaningful correlation. As mentioned above, Deleuze calls this possibility "*objectivism*":

> To be sensitive to signs, to consider the world as an object to be deciphered, is doubtless a gift. But this gift risks remaining buried in us if we do not make the necessary encounters; and these encounters would remain ineffective if we failed to overcome certain stock notions. The first of these is to attribute to the object the signs it bears...We think that the "object" itself has the secret of the signs it emits... For the sake of convenience, let us call *objectivism* this tendency (26).

When we associate the sign with one of the actions/thoughts surrounding its emergence, the sign becomes synonymous with it, such that existentially it "appears as the replacement of an action or thought", and thus as a replacement of their meaning before the mind (6). The associated action/thought signifies the sign, 'replacing' its existential call with a definite object.

However, the sense in which Deleuze uses the term 'replacement' in order to characterize this semiotic exchange is rather vague. On the one hand, it means that the sign "stands for action and for thought" (6), but this too seems equally obscure. If the sign stands for another action/thought, it can only be within a series of understanding, namely the series of that action/thought. This implies that the sign's impression somehow supplants an action/thought's place in our intellect, of which there are four possible effects:

1. The sign's impression joins the series of the action/thought, so that all its impression is understood within it. The sign is immediately 'meaningful' and immediately 'understood', aligning with that series such that it shares in its extended understanding. The sign does not displace the action/thought in that series, rather it merely 'replaces' the action/thought momentarily in our consideration of it, as we pass beyond the action/thought into this series of understanding, and bequeath it to the sign. The effect extends the meaning of that series by the affects of the sign, while these affects, in turn, become explicitly meaningful through the other materials of that series.

2. The sign's impression and its emotional and existential affects correlate to each other and form their own series. A new meaning is created for the meaningless sign, which begins an entirely new series of understanding in the intellect. The new series is thus assembled like a collage, extracting meanings from the previous, in addition to all other signs, meanings, and understandings available. When complete, the new series of understanding emerges in parallel to the old, which stands in its own right.

3. The sign's impression completely displaces an action/thought from its series of understanding. The usurped action/thought is rendered meaningless, consequently becoming a sign itself, prompting a new search. What was previously meaningful and understood is rendered meaningless, and vice-versa.

4. The sign's impression finds no meaning at all, but continues to disturb us, prompting perpetually new searches. Effectively, all affects of the sign become signs themselves that perpetually disturb our understanding. In effect, the sign and its affects are *associated* but never *correlated* to other materials. They infinitely keep signing.

So which of these effects does Deleuze have in mind when he speaks of 'objectivism?' In order to resolve this ambiguity, we need to consider the clues he has left us.

To begin with, objectivism is "to attribute to the object the signs it bears" (26). On the one hand, there is an object or impression (e.g. Proust's narrator's tea/cake), on the other, some feeling or affect that arises along side it (e.g. the emotions associated with them). Through a "tendency which is natural to us or, at least, habitual" (26), we hastily attribute this affect to the object that elicits it. The sign is both the action/thought it stands for, and the feelings it enunciates within us. These are brought together so that the one implies the other and vice-versa. Objectivism is therefore the tendency of a sign's affects to find meaning in the materials they are immediately associated with. Thus, in the four possible effects of the sign that we have already deduced, it is the second that pertains to 'objectivism' specifically. The sign's affects are immediately correlated to the action/thought associated with them. The two 'designate' each other, and give each other a basic meaning.

It is important to note that from a material realist perspective the impressions and affects of signs are as much materials as the actions/thoughts that they are associated with and correlated to. However, a sign's impression (whether emotional or sensitive) is, as of its emergence, meaningless. Nonetheless, this impression/material is progressing towards a correlation with others, which will give it meaning, and perhaps even lead towards a broader understanding of its significance. Let us now trace an example of this movement, with regards to the specific case of objectivism, wherein two simple impressions/ materials correlate.

Imagine before us a specific action or thought. Suddenly, this action/thought is imbued with an existential feeling, in ourselves and in our relation to it, which illuminates its presence before us and demands that we find a meaning for this feeling and this relation. There are three phenomena at play here: the action/thought, the feeling it generates, and the association of the feeling to the original action/thought, all of which are properly 'signs' insofar as they are searched. Signs are meaningless impressions, which then become meaningful through their association and correlation to each other. Different types of signs represent different types of associations and correlations. In objectivism, all three impressions correlate to each other so as to become a new object. The feeling produced by an action/thought correlates to that action/thought, giving it further meaning and distinguishing it from all other impressions, actions, and thoughts.

The designated object may then extend beyond this relation, correlating with other impressions or objects into further meaningful relations. By doing so, a designated object becomes a 'significant' object, signifying precisely those other impressions and objects to which it correlates. Here, we surpass basic meaning and begin to understand the object, for the search for meaning is not simply limited to designating objects. Objects are equally correlated to other impressions and meanings, allowing us to understand their wider relation to the world. This is a sign's 'significance', its broader meaning, wherein the affects of the sign not only designate the action/thought to which it was first associated, but signify completely different ones.

We must keep in mind, though, that objectivism does little to help us understand either the sign or its object. While remaining in this state, the sign is meaningful only in the sense of its object, which tells us nothing about it. It is as if the sign duplicates itself and its parts ad infinitum in a completely redundant meaning. To borrow an expression from Heidegger, "to name is to call and clothe something in a word", in this case the sign 'clothes' the object, thus designating it:

> When we name a thing, we furnish it with a name. But what about this furnishing? After all, the name is not just draped over the thing. On the other hand, no one will deny that the name is coordinated with the thing as an object. If we conceive the situation in this way, we turn the name, too, into an object. We see the relation between name and thing as the coordination of two objects. The coordination in turn is by way of an object, which we can see and conceive and deal with and describe according to its various possibilities. The relation between what is named and its question is whether this correctly conceived coordination will ever allow us, will allow us at all, to give heed to what constitutes the peculiar property of the name (Heidegger: 120).

We see here that the coordination of the sign and its object is an act, wherein the sign designates its object as much as the object designates it. However, the meaning of each is not extended beyond each other, beyond pure redundancy.

Why does this happen? What benefit could this possibly have for consciousness? To begin with, it creates a new object, which is still somewhat illuminated by its sign. Just because we have established a sign's object does not stop it from continuing to sign. Rather. it provides a frame of reference for its search, extending the sign's associations in and through the impressions and objects correlated to it, in addition to their respective associations and understandings. Searching the objective sign, we rummage through all these associations, extending its world by what we find there. The apparent redundancy of objectivism is actually an invitation to create a world of that object, rediscovering its materials in their own terms and understandings. This is why Deleuze calls objective signs "*worldly signs*" (Deleuze 1972: 6), because their meaning becomes a particular and exclusive world of that object simply by extending its correlations and meanings into a stable series of understanding. Remember, 'a world' is any consistent series of understanding whose objects and impressions correlate to each other in such a way as to preserve the same correlations to each other. Every object thus presents us with potential worlds, having a consistent meaning that is extended merely by searching it.

Designation vs. Signification; Perception vs. Intelligence

To understand a worldly sign only in terms of the materials from which it was composed is a rather poor articulation of its potential, for through objectivism we never learn that sign's significance, we only know its most basic meaning. It remains at the brute level of an object, without enunciating the relation of that object in terms of all the other impressions and actions/thoughts of which we are familiar. But if not a worldly meaning, how else can the sign be resolved?

Deleuze tells us that designation is only half of a sign's meaning, and that in addition to finding meaning in its own material, a sign may find meaning elsewhere. To understand a sign is to extend the meaning of a sign beyond its mere designation. And the moment we stray from the sign's designative sense, we are dealing with another type of sign, which makes the object a sign itself (viz. of other worlds) and prompts a different type of search.

Deleuze observes that the narrator in Proust is repeatedly "disappointed" by the objects before him:

> Disappointment is a fundamental moment of the search of apprenticeship: in each realm of signs, we are disappointed when the object does not give us the secret we were expecting... Disappointment on first hearing Vinteuil, on first meeting Bergotte, on first seeing the Balbec Church (33).

To remedy this situation, Proust's narrator searches for a "*subjective compensation*" to give these objects meaning beyond their raw existence. The objects are again embraced as signs, producing affections in excess of their objective dimension. These affects, which are distinct from the material and objective roots of their signs, nonetheless correlate to them, extending their worlds and giving them greater meaning. If this meaning is 'subjective', it is because it varies depending on the all the other objects and impressions it solicits, becoming 'subject' to all the worlds in which they partake.

In its own right, objectivism is certainly significant, but not all significations are objective. In fact, as we have argued, only the worldly signs are, for they ground the sign in the first material object associated to it. Meanwhile, this objective sense remains significant because it continues to sign and allude to other impressions and objects. In actuality, "we are disappointed when the object does not give us the secret we were expecting" (33). Again, think of all the narrator's disappointments (e.g. Vinteuil, meeting Bergotte, the Balbec church, meeting Mme. De Guermantes, etc.) (32-33).

Our disappointment lies in our realization that the object does not give us a sufficient understanding. Our search has been only partially resolved because the object itself now 'signs'. Disappointment is this existential state in which we find that our articulation of the sign is not enough to end our search. Instead, it is like a new search arrives immediately upon the old, the two propelling each other towards some other meaning. The object becomes a sign in its own right, and we are pushed beyond it towards a greater significance. And so, despite designating, the sign "*signifies* something different", through which it also approaches the " "truth" side" of itself that lets us "know" it beyond its raw existence (26).

In order to 'know' the sign we must further trace its relation to other objects, signs, and materials. We must actively form new series of understanding about the sign, so that its broader significance can be discovered. Yet the propensity towards objectivism, and against this activity of knowing signs, is still quite overwhelming. To prefer "the facility of recognitions" is a continual temptation (26). And no wonder:

> "Objectivism" spares no kind of sign. This is because it does not result from a single tendency, but groups a complex of tendencies. To refer a sign to the object which emits it, to attribute to the object the benefit of the sign, is first of all the natural direction of perception or of representation. But it is also the direction of voluntary memory, which recalls things and not signs. It is, further, the direction of pleasure and of

> practical activity, which count on the possession of things or on
> the consumption of objects. And in another way, it is the
> tendency of the intelligence. *The intelligence tends towards
> objectivity, as perception towards the object.* The intelligence
> dreams of objective content, of explicit objective significations
> which it is able, of its own accord, to discover or to receive or
> to communicate. The intelligence is thus objectivist, as much
> as perception. It is as the same moment that perception assigns
> itself the task of apprehending the sensuous object, and
> intelligence the task of apprehending objective significations.
> For perception supposes that truth is to be *spoken, formulated*
> (28).

Here, Deleuze distinguishes between 'perception' and
'intelligence', the primary tendencies of objectivism. Perception
is none other than the awareness and exchange of amorphous
materials. To perceive is to grasp and sift through the various
materials of the world in order to eventually have them before us
as objects. Insofar as these unformed materials and signs bear no
correlation to themselves or to others, *perception is entirely
meaningless.* As Hume pointed out, it does not lead to
understanding, rather "as far as the senses are judges, all
perceptions are the same in the manner of their existence"
(Hume: 187). Perception is merely our ability to distinguish
things in the world, and to associate them generally.

'Intelligence', on the other hand, is the 'natural' ability to
see these things as meaningful objects. Intelligence begins with
'objective content' and proceeds towards correlating these
objects to each other in 'objective significations'. Like an
unrestrained objectivism, intelligence finds no limit to what it
can signify, only limits between the significations themselves
(i.e. their various codes) and the objects available to
consciousness. Intelligence must therefore take all objects
themselves as signs, in order that they can designate ad
infinitum. Thus, it simultaneously grasps the object in two
senses: its objective designation, and its subjective
significance.[15]

---

[15] Hume similarly speaks of a difference in kind between perception and
"reasoning" (i.e. the act of forming intelligence) (77). For Deleuze and Spinoza's
take on 'Reason', see Chapter V.

The first "series" of significations that we encounter are the objects immediately perceived. But "we shall be lost, all our freedom lost, if we give the object the benefit of the signs and significations which transcend it" (Deleuze 1972: 30). If this were the case, there would be no more depth to truth than a bare recognition of objects. Understandings would never be assembled, for we would be deprived of any form of significance beyond immediate recognition and empirical association. All subjective intelligence would fail, and we would be unable, not only to abstract logical possibilities, but to imagine, dream, symbolize, or translate anything. A miserable existence indeed! And so, it is these subjective compensations, these abstract and imaginary possibilities, allow us to formulate different understandings of the same object, compounding our knowledge of the world.

However, before abandoning the worldly sign, we must not overlook its importance and what it allows us to do:

> The worldly sign does not refer to something, it "stands for" it, claims to be equivalent to its meaning. It anticipates action as it does thought, annuls thought as it does action, and declares itself adequate: whence its stereotyped aspect, and its vacuity. We must not thereby conclude that such signs are negligible. The apprenticeship would be imperfect, and even impossible, if it did not pass through them. These signs are empty, but this emptiness confers upon them a ritual perfection, a kind of formalism we do not encounter elsewhere (6-7).

The ability of the worldly sign to 'anticipate' and 'annul' action and thought is probably its most important trait. The worldly sign intervenes in an action/thought by re-opening it to worldliness. This anticipates new signs, and therefore it anticipates new relations of consciousness. If this 'annuls' action or thought, it is because it not only allows new signs to emerge, but allows us to forget the objects, actions, and thoughts from which they came so that we can concentrate on others and discover their meanings. If it 'anticipates' actions and thoughts, it is through the object that it instantiates, which is 'adequate' as a distinct and meaningful entity of consciousness, but which has an 'empty' or purely formal meaning, telling us nothing about its significance.

Devoid of necessary meaning, the worldly sign is searched among all the impressions at hand in our effort to articulate it. However, it may also fold back upon materiality in order to find new signs and impressions from which to draw its meaning. Thus, every encounter with a worldly sign is potentially a new search in which the sign at hand is erased by the emergence another. Worldly signs are perpetually changing:

> worldly signs, by virtue of their vacuity, betrayed something precarious or else have frozen already, immobilized in order to conceal their alteration. For worldliness, at each moment, is alteration, change (18).

If the worldly sign is precarious or even 'vacuous' on its own, the versatility of this sign is to blame. It literally begins like a vacuum in space, drawing in all sorts of signs, objects, and materials towards it in the desperate attempt to articulate its significance. Being no more than a raw material though, its search is easily usurped by these other signs and objects, while its significance is forgotten just as quickly as it emerged:

> Vacuity, stupidity, forgetfulness: such is the trinity of the worldly group. But worldliness thereby gains a speed, a mobility in the emission of signs, a perfection in formalism, a generality in meaning: all things which make it a necessary milieu for apprenticeship. As essence is incarnated evermore loosely, the signs assume a comic power…they excite the intelligence, in order to be interpreted. For nothing gives more food for thought than what goes on in the head of a fool… (80).

The worldly sign is so simple, and so devoid of meaning, that it approaches the pure act of apprenticeship and searching. The more one embraces worldly signs, the more one approaches pure semiosis and the emergence of signs in infinite relation. This is pure materiality and material relation, where all formed and unformed materials enter into flux with one another, bearing all possible relations with each other simultaneously. Knowledge is excited to its greatest degree, open to new meanings and signs from all directions.

But at the same time, there is certain degree of insanity and danger in such an open and liquefied semiosis. Everything becomes profound, but nothing means anything, as there is nothing but signs. These signs then collapse into one another, like a bad acid trip where everything is mashed in a synesthetic blend. Meanwhile, a mere movement away, these signs threaten to solidify themselves into significant relations again, but this time with no guarantee that they will not be so confused, so befuddled, that one descends into a paralyzing autism or schizophrenia.

To approach pure semiosis is a dangerous game, and yet we must draw near it to some extent in order to encounter the new. We must flirt with insanity, otherwise we would never learn nor apprentice to the unknown chaos that is the world. Worldliness is precisely the simultaneity of all signs, objects, and materials in all possible relations to each other: nonsense *par excellence*. Those that immerse themselves in it tread a dangerous line between nonsense and sense, like Nietzsche's tightrope walker, with death on all sides (Nietzsche 1969: 47-48).

In addition to absolute meaninglessness, there is another danger that the worldly sign presents. Deleuze notes that:

> the sign is doubtless more profound that the object emitting it, but it is still attached to that object, it is still half sheathed in it... (Deleuze 1972: 34-35).

The danger would lie in giving worldly signs nothing but their objective meaning and never understanding them at all. Thus, at one end of the spectrum we have the threat of absolute meaninglessness and the decent into complete chaos, while at the other we have the threat of an absolutely objective meaning and a completely superficial knowledge of the world.

We cannot overlook the fact that even at best the objective series is dissatisfying, and that worldly signs keep on 'signing' even after we have established and articulated their origin. And so, we must turn back towards the world so as to extend these objects, and to make further sense of their signs. The true Egyptologist continues to search, and, *"for the disappointment of the object, he attempts to find a subjective compensation"* (33). In effect, "we overcome the disappointment of the object by a compensation of the subject" (35). We fill in the vacuity of the object with other experiences and understandings. In so doing, we consider the sign without designation, or the sign blocked from its designative sense, signifying entirely different things and understandings.

This sign represents a different type than the worldly one. It is already more complex, prompting a multiplicity of different significations. Through it, we have become aware that the sign's object tells us nothing of its depth and meaning. This new type of sign draws us into all sorts of deceptions, hidden meanings, and worlds that no object can absolutely represent. Its mystery propels us into a madness that knows it will never have any 'objective' meaning, but which demands its significance despite it. This represents a world to which we have no access, and which keeps evading us every time we seem just about to grasp it. What a seductive play! Like postcards from a new world that is always just a little too far away. The more we try to reach it, the more signs it sends us. In the absence of any object, they can mean anything we want them to, like some fantasy run amok, or some passion unbound. How can we not fall in love with signs like these? How can we not desire these signs that give us everything we can imagine, asking only to be pursued?

B: Signs of Love (Subjective Signs)

Deleuze calls these other signs the "signs of love", for, as mentioned, they are best exemplified by the lovers of the *Search*. When Deleuze says that the signs of love "conceal what they express", and that their origins are "unknown", he means that their origins are somehow not present, and that they cannot therefore be reduced to an objective meaning (9). But how is this possible?

As we recall, the worldly sign emanates from materiality or from some action/thought already present to hand. Furthermore, it has a particular existential glint about it that prompts us to search its impression as a sign. As signs, these worldly impressions are composed of their own respective materials, distinct from all other actions/thoughts. Although these impressions may have risen out of some object, and therefore partake in some or all of the materials of that action/thought, these distinct portions functions dually. On the one hand, these worldly signs 'designate' their object through the matter or materials they share with it. On the other hand, these impressions 'signify' other materials and meanings. For the 'origins' of the signs of love to be 'concealed' or 'unknown', this second dimension must become the entire focus of consciousness. In other words, the material origin (i.e. the designation) of the sign of love is existentially blocked, and our attention is instead devoted entirely to its significance.

Now the sign, as mentioned, partakes in all or part of its material origin. But let us suppose that it were to only partake in part of this origin. Were the remainder to be 'lost' or 'forgotten' (which amount to the same thing relative to our search), the sign would continue to 'sign', but its designation would no longer be available. Or, on the other hand, if its origin is materiality itself, its origin would be completely amorphous and would designate no object, only the chaotic infinity of all impressions.

Its origin forgotten or indefinite, the sign of love is entirely significant. Until this origin is remembered or found, the sign is devoid of its objective ground and floats before consciousness in a vacuum, without recourse to the habitual and primary meaning of its designation. For now, this 'vacuity' can only be filled by finding an entirely significant meaning for the sign to compensate for lack of designation.

All cases of significance bear something of this 'loss' or 'forgetfulness'. It makes no difference whether the sign bears all or part of its material origin. What matters is that this original meaning (i.e. this designation) is dropped and replaced by a different material. The new material signifies the sign as much as the sign signifies it, and so both find new meaning in each other. In effect, we 'ignore' the origin and designation of the worldly sign in order to find its significance, and make it understood, for as mentioned, despite our habitual tendency to designate signs, these designations are ultimately dissatisfying, telling us nothing about the sign's broader meaning in the world. Looking for that significance, there is a different existential inclination at work, and therefore a different type of sign than the worldly one. In contrast to the worldly signs, the signs of love redistribute existential importance, turning our focus away from the sign's objective meaning towards its significance. Ironically, it is through our ignorance of the sign's objective and worldly meaning that we are lead towards an understanding of it. Until that point, these impressions remain entirely "stupid", having no other meaning beyond the redundancy of their objective sense (80).

Why call them 'signs of love' then? Why not just 'signs with concealed origins'? Keep in mind that Deleuze's concept of the sign is a refined version of Proust's, and in Proust these deceptive signs are most often conveyed through lovers, for one's beloved bears the signs of so many experiences of which their lover has no part. The origin of these signs is effectively lost because one's beloved has a past and present that is entirely their own. The fact remains that we are in perpetual ignorance of the other's phenomenological field, and of the greater part of their knowledge of the world. Thus, whenever one's love displays signs, one has only their personal experiences upon which to reflect. Consequently, one accounts for the signs of love force with imaginary and subjective ideas drawn entirely from one's own understandings and foreknowledge.

Before delving further into this idea, let us pause for a moment to offer one small critique of Deleuze's theory. As the signs of love are emitted from the body of one's beloved, there is always the chance that we may find an objective sense for these signs in that very body. This would be a rather superficial 'body language', or shall we say, a 'bodily significance' that would designate those signs in their material action. Instead of interpreting these signs as expressions of our beloved's private experiences, we can dispose ourselves towards them as if they have been 'made up on the spot' by that body, and have their immediate origin there. But does this argument hold? Can we really do this? It still seems somewhat dissatisfying, for we must then ask how it is that the body learned to compose itself in this significant way. Taking the whole body as a sign, we would still have to seek out the origins of the events from which it learned to compose itself. Once again we are led further back into the invisible worlds within our lover, and a past full of bodily events that are forever barred from us.

Accordingly, we can propose the following charitable interpretation of the ontology of the 'signs of love' that Deleuze omits. Deleuze never denies the materiality of the signs of love; in fact, he asserts it quite adamantly.[16] Being material, each sign of love designates an object. However, even though it is associated with an object, we cannot extract its significance from this designation, for the material of its object is also its own. This is part and parcel for our definition of significance, namely that it is meaning founded on the correlation of a sign to *other* signs and objects that are not part of its origin. A further corollary of this definition is that in order to do so a new existential relation must be entered into. Turning away from the designation of a sign means a new search, and therefore a new disposition towards understanding it, instead of merely designating it. This existential turn arises out of our feeling of dissatisfaction with a sign's designation. This feeling is itself another object, but not one that is an origin to the sign of love, but one that is produced by that very sign or object of love. Here we see that the worldly sign has surpassed itself, and has enunciated not only a demand for significance, but another feeling/sign of 'dissatisfaction' from out of materiality.

The signs of love are always coupled with "disappointment", which in its own right has its designation in the sign of love and its lack of significance (Deleuze 1972: 33). In order to resolve it, we must find new meanings for the signs of love, which, upon so doing, will simultaneously end our dissatisfaction and bear its significance. Yet, in order to find these meanings we have nothing other than the signs, actions, and thoughts already within our overall knowledge of the world, which painfully have already failed to explain this sign. If only these pains signified the signs of love, that would be the end of the matter. But they can only designate them, and compound our dissatisfaction further.

Unfortunately for us, the signs of love are already too complex. The lover reveals too many mysteries and too many 'almost familiar' signs for us to be satisfied considering them

---

[16] See "The Materiality of the First Three Types of Signs" below.

merely as objective signs of their body. And what poor readings of the other this would be if we did! This would be an extreme form of autism where people would be no different better off than thoughtless and lifeless moving objects. Surprisingly though, many discourses on love proceed in this way. Consider the various scientific analyses of love that attempt to break it down according to chemical processes and biological functions. Or consider those psychological discourses that try to give human actions a purely material significance. Only a little searching reveals to us the depth of our lover, and shows us the inadequacy of treating their signs in this way.

Existentially we suspect the signs of our love immediately, for the objects surrounding them insufficiently explain their meaning. Our dissatisfaction with them alerts us to the fact that their meaning resides somewhere in our beloved's private experience, from which we are obviously barred. Nevertheless, we fall back on our own experiences of the world and of our lover in order to try to subjectively compensate for this absence. We may never know our beloved's signs objectively, but we still desire a subjective approximation of their meaning, as well as a broader understanding of these signs and their relation to ourselves and to our world. We do not ask what the signs of love mean in themselves, but what they mean for us, as lovers of this person.

Yet, in searching the signs of love, we have only our understanding of the world from which to draw from. In the process of this subjective bricollage, we imagine an entire world for our beloved, but still within the confines of our own experiences. Thus, the signs of love force us outside of our regular understandings and into entirely different series of meaning, but still always with an air of dissatisfaction, for they are only the logical consequences of our previous ones. In this way, the signs of love lead us into new worlds, but ones that are entirely imaginary, remixed from our previous understandings.

Nonetheless, love forces us into new worlds and into different subjective associations. Love is therefore the collision and collusion of different worlds and subjectivities, which reconstitutes our own subjectivity, identity, and knowledge in order to accommodate the signs of our beloved. The search of signs of love effectively blends subjectivities and hybridizes worlds, such that it becomes difficult to demarcate exactly which belong to 'us' and which belong to our beloved. Instead of dealing with a single subject, in the signs of love we are always dealing with a multiplicity of subjective associations that retain their distinctions from each other, and therefore represent a multiplicity of subjectivities inside of us (Deleuze 1994: 75). Epistemologically, love makes us a schizophrenic mess of series that perpetually evolve and redistribute themselves according to every encounter with our beloved.

Whereas the worldly signs represent autistic worlds of simple meanings and basic objects, the signs of love signify complex worlds and alien subjectivities. Although blocked from their actual truth and worlds, they exert an effect on us that collaterally becomes another world in its own right, supervening our understanding. An encounter with a sign of love is a breach of our own subjectivity because we must recompose our subjective series in order to accommodate the foreign sign. To do so we must return to materiality, but a materiality now facilitated by our relation to the other and to the signs of love they emit. In the tender exchange between our beloved and ourselves, we recompose our understanding, which simultaneously recomposes our relation to materiality in general. This produces its own material effects (i.e. signs, actions, and thoughts) which will themselves have to be sorted out by our intellect.

Consequently, the signs of love actually succeed in blending subjectivities, for as the signs of love pass from one to the other it is as if a virtual subjectivity is momentarily founded between them. This virtual subjectivity is the properly schizophrenic relation of all possible subjective relations between us and our beloved in simultaneous reverberation. It occurs purely at the material level, where our worlds are colliding with our beloved's such that both give new meaning to each other and, in so doing, produce an entirely different relation to the world, invisible to the both of us, but expressed within us as the new signs and objects we perceive.

The confusion of subjectivities that occurs in the signs of love is somewhat of a paradox. On the one hand we retain our subjectivity through our prior understanding of the world. On the other hand, the signs of love initiate a search that breaks these series and exposes them to new meanings:

> There is, then, a contradiction of love. We cannot interpret the signs of a loved person without proceeding into worlds which have not waited for us in order to take form, which formed themselves with other persons, and in which we are at first only an object among the rest (Deleuze 1972: 8).

What Deleuze should say is that there are *multiple* contradictions of love. First, in the fact that our subjectivity extends outside itself—into the signs of the other and into the materiality of the search—only to reconstitute itself again from those signs and materials. Without losing itself, our subjectivity extends, but also changes the sum of all its relations in that extension, remaining understood to itself, while at the same time not understanding the source of this growth (i.e. the worlds of the other, in addition to all the other worlds that exist in materiality).

Second, as Deleuze mentions in this passage, there is a contradiction in the fact that we are compelled to understand the signs of love, and yet we can never truly or objectively understand them because we are forever blocked from their origins. Instead, the signs of love find their significance in what we already know, so that all they succeed in doing is signifying oneself to oneself. Contradictorily, we search the signs of love in order to understand the other, and instead we end up understanding only ourselves. The signs of love, just like the worldly signs before them, are redundantly meaningful, yet unlike worldly signs, the signs of love have multiple senses, logically compounding our series of understanding. They refine the senses of understanding and extend our worlds, even though they take us no further than familiar impressions.

Thirdly, in blending our understandings, the signs of love frustrate and aggravate us, for despite these new understandings, we still have not attained the truth of their sign. In realizing this, we become jealous of our beloved, for only they know origins of their signs, and the hidden meaning we are looking for:

> The contradiction of love consists of this: the means we count
> on to preserve us from jealousy are the very means which
> develop that jealousy, giving it a kind of autonomy, of
> independence with regard to our love (8-9).

The signs of love exasperate our frustration because they
compound our misunderstandings of what they truly mean.
When we realize that the signs of love have no origin, we realize
that they represent a perpetual search that could hypothetically
signify anything. Their independence is both the infinite things
they signify, and their freedom from any origin that would end
this search and ground them in an objective meaning. This
tendency is what Deleuze calls the "first law of love":

> The first law of love is subjective: subjectively, jealousy is
> deeper than love, it contains love's truth. This is because
> jealousy goes further in the apprehension and interpretation of
> signs. It is the destination of love, its finality. Indeed, it is
> inevitable that the signs of a loved person, once we "explicate"
> them, should be revealed as deceptive: "addressed to us,
> applied to us, they nonetheless express worlds which exclude
> us and which the beloved will not and cannot make us know"
> (9).

Jealousy contains the depth of the search itself, for it continues
to obsessively interpret and reinterpret the signs of love. This
ensures that our sensitivity to the beloved's signs is sustained,
and that the broadest interpretation of our beloved can be made.
This is why jealousy is so much better at approaching the truth
of the signs of love: in jealousy, the lover mistrusts every
meaning they find for their beloved's signs. They perpetually
refuse to believe that they understand their lover, or that they
have 'figured their lover out', denying their own interpretations
of their love, as well as those their beloved gives them. Every 'I
love you' is taken as a lie, for each lover knows that there will
always be some degree of betrayal between them, as their
private experiences cannot ever be completely conveyed to the
other. In this sense, "The interpreter of love's signs is necessarily
the interpreter of lies" (9). The jealous lover is well aware that
the signs of love have no origin, and that attempt to supplement
that origin is already false.

Moreover, love abounds with the infinite: senseless and insensitive actions and words, meaningless looks and touches, unspecific thoughts and feelings, forgotten pasts, and unknown futures. Every lover is well aware of all the signs of love that both they and their beloved do not know the meaning of. Lacking origins, these signs express a love that is never objective but infinitely meaningful, provoking great "pain" as they lead us only towards the perpetually dissatisfaction with their meaning (12).

Jealousy "is the very delirium of signs", for the lover can interpret the meaningless signs of their beloved in such a way as to give them too much meaning (122). They can ascribe a hidden significance to every one of their acts, and attribute to them ultimate betrayals or ultimate satisfactions:

> The jealous man experiences a tiny thrill of joy when he can decipher one of the beloved's lies, like an interpreter who succeeds in translating a complicated text, even if the translation offers him personally a disagreeable and painful piece of information (15).

The lover never really 'deciphers' the hidden worlds of their lover, for these worlds are not their privilege. Even when they find the 'truth' of one of their lover's lies, they must realize that it is still their own subjective interpretation of that truth, and that the event in question holds a completely different significance for their beloved than it does for them. They only think that they have deciphered the lie, that is, they create a purely subjective meaning for it, letting their actions and thoughts follow from this fiction as if it were objective fact. The pleasure here belongs not only to understanding the lie, but to a certain vanity. The lover flatters him/herself as being so clever that they can actually glimpse the hidden worlds of their beloved and know them better than they know themselves.

Yet, there is nothing more to this than delirious fantasy. The more the lover wanders into such misapprehension, the more they approach a paranoia that can hardly be called love. They reach the point where everything must have meaning, and where all meanings point towards a betrayal of them by their beloved. They begin to feel that their beloved is 'cheating' on them, that their beloved shares secret signs and understandings with others. But isn't this always the case? For, as we have seen, whatever significance one finds in another is not the same as that which they find, for they are composed in different worlds and different subjectivities.

Other than this paranoia of love, there is also a lover's delirium that interprets the signs of the beloved with too much affection. These people 'read too much' into their love, subjectively attributing all the signs of their beloved's hidden worlds as being representative of mysterious affections. They interpret their beloved's past as being a past that was always already a preparation for them, and for their love. Meanwhile, they overestimate their beloved's feelings for them and imagine that their beloved loves them far beyond what they really do, or what they have actually expressed. Once again, we have a form of narcissism at work here, for these feelings have been subjectively created by the lover and attributed to themselves through the vehicle of their beloved. Their beloved has become a mere crutch, a mere prop for themselves which they impose imaginary affects upon so as to bolster their own ego. Meanwhile, in order to do so they have betrayed their own existence by denying their own infinity, claiming to know themselves through the other, and through the affections they hypothesize.

In understanding the worlds and souls of our beloved, we must be wary of the dangers of love. Paranoiac and delirious loves just go to show that our beloved's worlds can actually overwhelm our own, to the point where they may literally be the death of us. Love is always threatening and violent, for it usurps our mind and body and exposes them to new signs and relations that will irreparably change our very being. The fine line between a love that extends our understanding and a love that subdues it is never objectively clear until after we have already consumed those signs of our beloved.

In contrast, the wise lover knows how to take their beloved's signs in stride. If their beloved really is letting them down, they know that they can only wait until the object of that betrayal is revealed. They realize that there is always a degree of helplessness in love, a perpetual anxiety that stems from the trust they place in their beloved and the hope that they will not break this pact. And so the wise lover embraces a healthy degree of jealousy that comes from understanding that everyone (including their beloved) will understand their love differently than they do, and that love is never completely understood by anyone for that reason. This kind of lover embraces the fact that their beloved holds infinite and inaccessible signs. In fact, this is precisely what they love about them, for together their differences perpetuate each other's searches and in so doing propagate the living exchange of satisfactions and dissatisfactions that are the act of love as much as the act of learning itself.

Although barred from the origins of the lover's signs, we nonetheless observe recognizable patterns of behavior that betray the consistency of their origins. The lover knows that these patterns "refer to ghosts, to Third Parties, to Themes which are incarnated in himself according to complete laws" (30). However, lacking those origins that would confirm them objectively, these patterns and their signs are only subjectively understood. There are three possible outcomes here:

1. The sign is amalgamated into a series that we already understand and are familiar with, thus adding to our knowledge of it. Intelligence and understanding are increased, and the broader meaning of the sign is realized in the context of all our other understandings of the world.

2. The sign is unfamiliar, and cannot be explained with the knowledge and understanding at our disposal. In this case, a whole new series must be created in order to account for this sign. The sign becomes a basis for its own series, and is used as the origin of a new series of understanding (i.e. a new world for us to explore). Hence, the unfamiliar sign represents an entirely other world that we must expound upon by expanding our own subjective understanding to accommodate it. In effect, our subjectivity multiplies, as we create a place for this 'other' sign, in its own

world/subjective series. This in turn requires a retreat back into worldliness so that we can discover the new objects and signs that will populate this world.

3. Or, the sign does both, creating a new world, but also enriching the worlds we are already familiar with. Meanwhile, the series retain their independence from each other, and semiotically function according to their own distinct codes.

In all three cases, love forces us out of our particular world views back into the process of learning.

Ultimately then, the subjective process of trying to understand the 'themes' and 'laws' of the signs of love adds to our overall knowledge and intelligence. In its own way, love makes us more intelligent, luring us into apprenticeships with unknown worlds:

> To fall in love is to individualize someone by the signs he bears or emits. It is to become sensitive to these signs, to undergo an apprenticeship to them ...The beloved appears as a sign, a "soul": the beloved expresses a possible world unknown to us, implying, enveloping, imprisoning a world which must be deciphered, that is, interpreted. To love is to try to *explicate*, to *develop* these unknown worlds which remain enveloped within the beloved (7).

To love is to be open to signs, to explore signs, and to be willing to accept that although we may not understand them initially, they will acquaint us with new worlds and understandings. The more alien the world or worlds of the other, the more signs they emit relative to our own world, and the more our own world must be bent in order to understand them. Is it any wonder that so many loves end up in disaster? Our love becomes unbearable when we cannot adapt quickly enough or thoroughly enough to the signs of our lovers and they threaten to overwhelm our own world, reshaping it in such a way that we cannot bear the consequences.

Love is utterly frustrating in these regards. When we do not find those worlds, or when we find those worlds blocked, we cannot help but feel rejected. In this way, the signs of love can be as "disappointing" as the worldly signs (33). Instead of understanding our lover like we hoped, we arrive at so many betrayals: a past we cannot share, loves for others, and experiences and feelings that we can never know. And we cannot escape some degree of jealousy for all these reasons.

We can curb love's disappointment by being open to the worlds of our lover, and by accepting that we will never completely understand them. The signs of love give our beloved meanings above and beyond the objective, in a plurality of worlds that we would otherwise be ignorant of. Seduced by these, we find all sorts of signs that we were hitherto unacquainted with, which we then harmonize with our knowledge, in a symbiosis of worlds.

In this way, a sign of love always has a life of its own. It represents an unknown disposition towards the world, an unknown reality that we have yet to explore and unfold. Deleuze has even gone so far as to call it a "soul". What a daring way to conceive of not only the sign, but of our lovers! Not only do they represent individual realities and "*possible worlds*" (8), but a variety of tiny souls inhabiting them. Our lovers are like entire universes, filled with a multiplicity of worlds and souls that compound into the individual we love.

The signs of love betray a continuum of new signs and significations, behind whatever subjective understanding we have of them. Through our jealousy, any meaning they have one moment is undone the further we search, for "love unceasingly prepares its own disappearance, acts out its own dissolution" (17). On the one hand, because our beloved continually reveals more signs, forcing us to recompose our understanding of them. On the other hand, the signs of love are infinitely meaningful because their origins are lost, and their truth cannot be established. Therefore, the signs of love are perpetually insignificant, senseless, and meaningless. Love is infinite. Never are the lies of love so clear than when we consider love as having a complete sense, significance, or meaning (i.e. when we try to objectify our lover completely). And yet, as Sartre has well shown, intersubjectivity is such that just as soon as we think we have understood our lover they do something to defy that understanding, revealing worlds that we can never know (Sartre 1994: 379-412).

The signs of love bring us to a different boundary, where designation gives way to signification, and where objectivity and subjectivity give way to new and extraneous significations. Our jealous searches betray an unlimited supply of signs, objects, and meanings residing beyond our understanding of ourselves and others, in worlds foreign to our own. New knowledge awaits us in these other realms, but to ground them, and end our dissatisfaction with worldly signs and signs of love, we must assume another existential disposition, and search yet another kind of sign.

C: The Sensuous Signs (Qualitative Signs)

The worldly signs reveal an immediate meaning, designating themselves in their own material originsand creating objects from them. The signs of love, meanwhile, do not have these origins at their disposal, and so find subjective meaning by correlating to other objects of the understanding. In this correlation, our worlds are breached by materiality in order to accommodate these unfamiliar signs and produce meanings for them. Through this rupture of our worlds, new impressions are created, as our beloved's worlds collide with our own and we perceive their difference as so many new feelings, sensations, and unfamiliar signs. These are all appended to the sign of love and thus designate it, but they supersede it by also designating other objects and therefore worlds other than those of our beloved. Unlike the signs of love, these signs claim multiple origins, signifying both familiar and unfamiliar worlds. Beyond objective and subjective meaning is an entirely different type, simultaneously circulating in multiple worlds:

> The third world is that of sensuous impressions or qualities... the sign of an *altogether different* object which we must try to decipher, at the cost of an effort which always risks failure. It is as if the quality enveloped, imprisoned the soul of an object

other than the one it now designates. We "develop" this quality, this sensuous impression, like a tiny Japanese paper which opens under water and releases the captive form... First a prodigious joy, so that these signs are already distinguished from the preceding ones by their immediate effect. Further, a kind of obligation is felt, the necessity of a mental effort: to seek the sign's meaning... Then, the sign's meaning appears, yielding to us the concealed object... (Deleuze 1972: 11-12)

The worldly sign designates a single object that is its origin. This origin becomes its 'objective' sense, and the two articulate each other in a worldly signification. The signs of love once designated too, but their objective origins are no longer available, being lost, forgotten, or ignored. They can only correlate to the objects we know, signifying subjective understandings. Meanwhile, between both of these objective and subjective meanings other sensations arise. Materiality is such that as we search worldly signs and signs of love, new signs appear along-side them. These have origins in and through those objective and subjective meanings, and on that account at least they designate them. They bring with them a 'prodigious joy' because of their immediate designation, however just like any worldly sign they inevitably disappoint, for this meaning is redundant and superficial, signifying nothing but some object or understanding already known.

Instead, if these impressions are searched, we can surpass their familiar meaning and understand them in addition to their objective and subjective senses. Unlike the signs of love, these sensuous signs still designate their origins, and thus have immediate objective sense. But simultaneously they surpass this sense, for they designate *multiple* objects and claim all of them equally as their designation. The more we search them, the more objects we find for them, which not only add to their significance, but become the basis for their own searches and series of understanding. For instance, in the *Search* the narrator's love of the name Guermantes implies a range of things: the memory of the Guermantes way; the social worlds of the Hotel de Guermantes; the opera; Mme. de Villeparisis's; not to mention Mme. de Guermantes style of dress, and different ways of conducting herself (Proust I: 188, 235-262). The 'place-name'

Guermantes is not just an object of a subjective infatuation, but the sign and quality of all these strange worlds.

The sensuous signs designate and are designated by multiple objects. Because of this tendency, they extend even further, allowing all these objects to signify each other through this common sensation. The search of sensuous signs therefore allows us to understand series in terms of each other, and to exchange meanings between them, as we jump from series to series. And so, Deleuze denotes these sensuous signs 'qualities' insofar as they are shared between objects and understandings and signify multiplicities of them (11).

When Deleuze says that it is "as if the quality enveloped, imprisoned the soul of an object other than the one it now designates" (11), he means that we are unable to distinguish an ideal origin for the sensuous sign. The sensuous sign not only signifies multiple objects, but designates all of them too. These objects thus share and lay claim to the same sensuous sign, which acts as generalized attribute of them all. This shared quality partakes in all their respective series at the same time, while also creating a tacit link from each to each in a network of series. Embracing and searching qualities, one can insinuate all sorts of subjective associations, as these different series signify each other through their shared quality. Consequently, their codes get mixed and entirely new series of understanding are created between them.

Sensuous signs are entirely simulacral in that they have no definite origin. Rather, they partake in multiple origins and therefore have multiple instances. Beyond all objects and series they signify, they continue to allude to others, for they have no definite sense. In this respect, the sensuous signs are similar to the signs of love, representing displaced objects and origins that we can only subjectively hypothesize. However, they differ from the signs of love in that they nonetheless have other origins and senses:

> This is because the sensuous qualities or impressions, even properly interpreted, are not yet in themselves adequate signs. But they are no longer empty signs, giving us a factitious exaltation like the worldly signs. They are no longer deceptive signs which make us suffer, like the signs of love whose real

meaning prepares an ever greater pain. These are true signs which immediately give us an extraordinary joy, signs which are fulfilled, affirmative and joyous (12-13).

Instead of a single origin or single meaning, the sensuous signs represent infinite origins and multiple understandings. If they are not 'adequate' in themselves, it is because they do not have a single definite origin, but infinite origins, meaning any search of them can be equally infinite and unending. Yet, they are more than just 'empty signs', immediately giving us the joy of multiple objective meanings. They prompt us to continue searching for more of these, as we realize that all these objects and all our understandings of them – whether objective or subjective – signify even more, and therefore there is no limit to the joys they can bring.

The Materiality of the First Three Types of Signs

Throughout *Proust and Signs*, Deleuze repeatedly emphasizes the materiality of the worldly sign, the sign of love, and the sensuous sign. With the worldly sign, this is quite obvious, for the worldly sign is still attached to its object, and still "half sheathed in it" (34-35). The materiality of the worldly sign is already along-side it, the ground of its very significance. The materiality of this sign corresponds directly with the materiality of its origin, so that both of them signify each other and the sign has meaning. The material of both origin and sign are never in doubt, as the sign is no more than a repetition of all or part of that materiality within us.

In the case of the sign of love, its origin is concealed, but the sign is nonetheless material, bearing some part of this concealed material origin, and now a different material object in its own right. In our attempt to remedy this situation, we give this sign "a subjective interpretation, in which we reconstruct associative series" (34). These "subjective chains of association" reconstruct the missing origins of the sign of love by positing hypothetical *material* origins in their place (36). Thus, the signs of love are material in their immediate communication (i.e. their 'signing') and in their significance, which come from materials already known.

As for the sensuous signs, they too remain material:

> Not simply by their sensuous origin. But their meaning, as it is developed, signifies Combray, young girls, Venice, or Balbec. It is not only their origin, it is their explanation, their development which remains material (12).

We search the sensuous signs until their "hidden meaning appears, yielding to us the concealed object[s] – Combray for the madeleine, young girls for the steeples, Venice for the cobblestones..." (11-12). Every sensuous quality stretches between multiple material objects, acting as an objective sign of them all.[17] Qualities are similar to the worldly signs in that their material origins are immediate. Above the objects they immediately designate, they also subjectively relate to the series of understanding that all these objects belong to, in an abundance of material implications:

> These are true signs which immediately give us an extraordinary joy, signs which are fulfilled, affirmative and joyous. *But they are material signs.* Not simply by their sensuous origin. But their meaning, as it is developed, signifies Combray, you girls, Venice, or Balbec. It is not only their origin, it is their explanation, their development which remains material (12-13).

The immediate joy of the sensuous sign lies in its objectivity and its abundant designations. But the sensuous signs differ in kind

---

[17] Notice how Deleuze equates 'sensuous origin' with materiality. Here, as in his other writings, Deleuze reveals his empirical leanings. Deleuze is strictly a material realist; however this material realism quickly gives way to an empirical reality in the Essence of our being. Empirical sensations and impressions *are* materials, namely materials of the mind and body, which correlate into the various objects and understandings that we know. This is not the place to discuss the ontological arguments for this in detail, suffice to say the empirical/materialism of Deleuze is thoroughly discussed elsewhere (i.e. in *Logic of Sense*, *Empiricism & Subjectivity: An Essay on Hume's Theory of Human Nature*, and *Francis Bacon: The Logic of Sensation*). However it is important to consider that for Deleuze, memories, imaginations, feelings, and other sensations are completely material entities differentiated entirely within a material ontology that we will discuss more in Part II.

from the worldly, having a multiplicity of objective meanings and never just one. Although they are *true* signs, obviously designating particular things, they are "inadequate" (12), stretching beyond their objective meaning into objects and worlds not yet encountered. Intensively and extensively, the sensuous signs are infinitely meaningful: intensively, through all the objects and significations they mean; extensively, because the sensuous signs have a power far greater than these meanings, implicating other signs and understandings that have yet to be discovered.

At this point, several things are becoming apparent in Deleuze's theory. Not only are the worldly signs, the signs of love, and the sensuous signs material, but they are all converging in sensuality. First, consider the worldly signs. The worldly signs are separated from the sensuous signs merely by an existential disposition. The moment we become dissatisfied with a sign's objective meaning is the moment we must consider the worldly sign as a quality, not only of that dissatisfaction, but of other objects and worlds. We begin looking for that sign elsewhere, in other objects and in other associations of objects. And so, the worldly sign is actually just a rather naïve way of grasping the sensuous sign, which locks the sign into just one origin and one designation. Worldly signs allow us to 'sense' their origins, but through that immediate meaning we are blocked from the 'sensuality' of their sign (i.e. their potential to find this sense elsewhere in other objects, and in other series of meaning). Yet, with only a little searching, our imagination and our memory begin to associate these worldly signs with a whole host of other materials beyond one origin. For example: the circumstances in which it was discovered and all the various objects surrounding it; the feelings that worldly object dredges up for us (whether they be joys or disappointments); hypothetical and imaginary objects that partake in that sign and give it a subjective meaning; and other "union[s] of ideas".[18] Only a bit of searching is sufficient to transform that worldly sign into a sensuous one, and to extend its significance into others (as objective or subjective as they may be).

---

[18] The expression is borrowed from Hume, who likewise shows how the imagination unites ideas together into various systems of belief (Hume: 94).

Meanwhile, the signs of love are also a naïve way of grasping what could be a sensuous sign. It is all a matter of perspective. Finding their meaning in subjective associations, the signs of love draw their significance from objects and signs we already know. Now, as every object the sign of love correlates to is composed of other impressions, every sign of love therefore signifies all of these simultaneously and conjunctively. Each sign of love, therefore, becomes a quality of them that we are free to search and attribute to an infinite multiplicity of objects.

Thus, in both the case of the worldly sign and the case of the sign of love, all it takes is a return to the search so as to extend their relations and turn them into sensuous signs. The moment we are dissatisfied with the worldly, each sign of love becomes a quality of both that dissatisfaction and its object. While the moment the sign of love signifies an object, it becomes a quality of the respective impressions and relations of that object.

Considered as a sensuous sign, the worldly sign always has one significance turned towards its origin (i.e. its objective significance), the other towards its potential to be a quality to some other material(s) (i.e. its subjective significance). Meanwhile, the sign of love always signifies its displaced origins, which cannot be resolved, making it instead the quality of other familiar materials. Thus, the ideal origin of the worldly sign is shattered by its potential to be a quality, while the ideal origin of the sign of love is shattered by its 'becoming-quality' to other subjective associations. And yet the ideal origin of the sensuous sign is also shattered by its multiple origins just as well as its multiple 'becoming-qualities' to other materials. All three, in light of the search, fail to secure their ideal origins and instead become the qualities of so many origins, so many materials. Consequently, at the level of their materiality, the worldly sign, the sign of love, and the sensuous sign are not resolved in some ideal origin or origins, but in the infinite meaning and significance of materiality and all the signs, actions, and thoughts therein. Neither the worldly sign nor the sign of love represent *ideal origins*, it is rather that they represent *ideal essences* that both designate and signify themselves.

The ideality of the sign falls apart in light of the fact that all signs find meaning in objects and all objects find further meaning in each other, such that every sign is expressed in an infinite number of significant relations. Thus, at the ontological level, the materiality of the worldly signs, the signs of love, and the sensuous signs, makes all of them 'qualities' of each other, infinitely related. While epistemologically, signs are fundamentally without an absolute meaning on this account, unlimited in their significance and therefore all qualities before they are ever worldly signs or signs of love.

Relative to the search (which we must remember is ontologically prior to all signs), the sign has infinite meaning and continues to signify and remain a quality of other signs and materials. Meanwhile:

> At the end of the Search, the interpreter understands what had escaped him... that the material meaning is nothing without an ideal essence which it incarnates. The mistake is to suppose that the hieroglyphs represent "only material objects." But what now permits the interpreter to go further is that meanwhile the problem of art has been raised, and has received a solution. Now the world of art is the ultimate world of signs, and these signs, as though *dematerialized*, find their meaning in an ideal essence. Henceforth, the world revealed by art reacts on all the others, and notably on the sensuous signs; it integrates them, colors them with an aesthetic meaning and imbues what was still opaque about them. Then we understand that the sensuous signs *already* referred to an ideal essence which was incarnated in their material meaning. But without art we should not have understood this, nor transcended the law of interpretation... This is why all the signs converge upon all apprenticeships, by the most diverse paths, are already unconscious apprenticeships to art itself. At the deepest level, the essential is in the signs of art (13).

The three types of material signs do not converge upon a material meaning (i.e. some origin, or some absolute significance), but insinuate an ideal meaning that is completely immaterial. Ontologically speaking, all signs are signs of a primordial materiality, which is the sum of all materials, without being any specific one. Inhering within materiality are those essences that are virtual, but which divide materiality into specific signs and their relations. These essences are immaterial insofar as they never adhere to a specific material, but express an infinite multiplicity of materials, drawn from the substratum of materiality itself. In *Proust and Signs*, Deleuze holds off on the specific arguments for these dynamic processes, instead giving an existential argument for their existence.[19]

To start with, Deleuze recognizes that whenever Proust's narrator is in the presence of art and tries to contemplate the meaning of a work of art, an altogether different sign is at work. Art fails to resolve itself in an ideal origin, rather the more the work is surveyed, the more qualities and meanings it takes on. Regardless of its form or media, art leads us to these radical transformations and creations, which change our worlds and divulge a productive essence that surpasses all our understanding. Evolving as they do, works of art cannot be ideally signified by any of these understandings, which holistically function together, so as to give the work of art infinite sense.[20]

It makes no difference whether we search the objects or the qualities of the work of art first, for all them extend infinitely, in and through each other and all their relations. Art remains infinitely meaningful. And so we must ask, where does the search of the work of art leads us? Where is the truth of the work of art? Holistically expressed by this infinite multiplicity of material signs and significations, its truth is not in any one of them absolutely, but in all of them collectively, and infinitely. The truth of the work of art is therefore an infinite and ideal essence that inheres within all of these materials, but which exceeds their materiality.

The sensuous signs brought us closest to this immaterial realm. Considering that there is no necessary end to either their objective or subjective meanings, there is similarly no end to their materiality. Their truth resides in something completely immaterial about them, which allows them to signify indefinitely. In their infinite meaning, qualities allude to the

---

[19] Specifically, these arguments will begin in *Difference and Repetition* and *Expressionism in Philosophy: Spinoza*, and will continue in his subsequent works.

[20] For a detailed study of the infinite sense of art see Nancy's *The Muses* (Nancy 1996).

immaterial production of meaning, the self-organizing patterns inhering within materiality itself that create all these disparate objects and significant orders, and which lend their power to the existential search positing them. In as much as they do so, the sensuous signs converge upon art, their series becoming a creative work of art in itself. *Therefore, the pursuit of a quality, at its extreme limit, is art, and vice versa: art is the pursuit of qualities.*

D: The Signs of Art
(Essential Signs)

As signs emerge from out of materiality, they signify the powers of materiality, whose chaotic relations congeal into distinct signs and materials. The amorphous becomes the distinct, just as the distinct but meaningless becomes the significant and meaningful – all through causes that we neither know nor understand. We are unable to grasp these genetic powers of materiality as specific objects, and yet they create and give forth all objects. In other words, art becomes distinct signs and significations, however art is never arrived at distinctly or significantly. If it was, art would become absolute, which is to say it would become objective. Yet, whatever is objective is neither creative nor artistic, for having already arrived at its meaning and significance it neither becomes nor solicits the new, being always already the object that it is.

In art we find a plethora of signs and materials at play with one another, each of which are signs of that art. In ontological priority, all worldly, subjective, and sensuous signs are first signs of art, signs of an invisible genesis, however none of them are the object, ground, or absolute meaning of this art producing them. While holistically expressing it and signifying it, they cannot do so absolutely, nor render this art a simple object or significance. Whatever we understand or know of an art is only a shadow of it: a significance that is expressed by it, or a sign which signifies it, but never an object that captures art's activity finitely. Thus in art, there is an ontological divide of two different levels: one distinct and significant; the other virtual and immanent to those distinctions, signified by the former, without becoming significant itself. Or should we say that there are three levels: the virtual and insignificant (i.e. art); the distinct and signifying (i.e. signs); and the distinct and significant (i.e. meanings/objects).

In the discovery of art, whose signs have no definite origin or signification, our search leads us beyond material signs into materiality itself as the fountainhead of all distinct materials and significations. Searching the signs of art, we posit our search entirely within those breaches of our knowledge wherein new signs are emerging and trying to get at their immaterial source:

> Now the world of art is the ultimate world of signs, and these signs, as though *dematerialized*, find their meaning in an ideal essence...Then we understand that the sensuous signs *already* referred to an ideal essence which was incarnated in their material meaning. But without art we should not have understood this, nor transcended the law of interpretation which corresponded to the analysis of the madeleine. This is why all the signs converge upon art; all apprenticeships, by the most diverse paths, are already unconscious apprenticeships to art itself. At the deepest level, the essential is in the signs of art (Deleuze 1972: 13).

If the world of art is the ultimate world of signs, it's because all along it has been *the* world, the very materiality through which all worlds are differentiated and in which all worlds gather their respective materials and understandings. This world of art is populated by 'ideal essences' which express in the concrete as the distinct signs, objects, and significations that we encounter.

Ideal essence, in art as well as in general, has been alluded to all along by Deleuze and Proust. All three types of material signs have hinted at them, and "we learn that they *already* incarnated, that they were already there in all these kinds of signs, in all the types of apprenticeship" (Deleuze 1972: 36-37). We see their influence most particularly in the case of the search of sensuous signs. Qualities are embodied materially by objects that contain them as a property. But the object is as much a property of the quality, as the quality is a property of the material object. As this quality is a property of an infinite series of material objects and relations, through this quality, and all its other qualities, the material object likewise signifies an infinite series of other objects. Deleuze is thus tacitly arguing that the qualities do not necessarily belong to their objects; while similarly, objects do not necessarily belong to their qualities. Rather, every object and quality just happens to temporally correlate in order to give each other meaning. In the span of time, we cannot say of any material object that it will retain any quality. Thus, qualities – and the objects that embody them – are completely *coincidental*. But this coincidence in turn leads us to the ideality of the quality. Wherefore the coincidence? It must reside in an immaterial essence, which inheres within these materials indistinctly, organizing their correlation without being represented. This meaning of meaning, this ideal power of correlation, is entirely virtual and immaterial, and yet it is the *instance* of the quality, its object, and their infinite correlation (i.e. *co*-incidence).

The signs of art, on the other hand, reveal these infinite powers even better, as they over-brim with new signs and meanings, and immediately reveal materiality's creative powers. In Deleuze's words:

> What is the superiority of the signs of art over all the others? It is that the others are material...*Only the signs of art are immaterial* (39).

Whereas the sensuous signs lead us from their quality to the infinite multiplicity of objects that bear them, the signs of art instead lead us to the 'production' of infinite signs, objects, and worlds. The search of art actually produces new materials and material relations, as we touch upon infinite creation and genesis through it, which is to say, the insignificant practice of distinguishing and understanding the world. Not only does it distinguish the various signs and impressions that we perceive, it imbues these perceptions with meaning and significance by correlating them to each other.[21]

Unfortunately though, our subjective attempts to understand these essences seldom discover their power, and fail to creatively inspire us:

---

[21] Were it not for this power, we could neither understand nor know, but would be left in a completely intuitive and reactive existence; sensitive, but only instinctively so.

> Far from leading us to a true appreciation of art, subjective
> compensation ends by making the work of art itself into a mere
> link in our associations of ideas (35).

The work of art is passed off as any other object, given a general meaning and superficial reflection. We make the grave epistemological mistake of believing that we have understood the piece of art and that we have figured out its intention, or the intention of its creator. These convictions only come when we have turned away from our search of art's signs, preferring to grasp it as something familiar and banal, rather than as a dynamic and powerful force.

However, beyond all objective meanings we must inquire into the origins of the work of art, the creative process that made it. Art gives us a glimpse of the powers of creativity, leading us into a more profound search that touches upon the essences of its materials, and which continues to produce new interpretations. We grasp the work of art again, differently this time, as filled with qualities signifying infinite relations to other objects, as well as entirely immaterial relations to ideal essences. Our search pushes into the source of all meaning, into the pure signifiance of the sign without limit. Consequently, we pass through the sensuous signs into the signs of art, which are more like signs that infinitely lead back to signs, and into the complex play of all their objective and subjective meanings in entirely different worlds. In sum, the worldly signs, the signs of love and the sensuous signs become objects and understandings, while the signs of art produce these signs, objects, and understandings. *Art is the production of semiosis, the birth of signs, and the cause of all their relations.*

Essence as Style and Viewpoint

As we can see, the signs of art are much more complex than the other types of signs. Beyond purely objective, subjective, and material meanings, art propels us into ideal essences, multiple worlds, and infinite searches. More than just a collection of materials, art is the method through which we seize upon the creative power of materiality itself and utilize this power to create the new. "Essence is always an artistic essence" (50), which is to say, what is essential is infinitely creative, becoming worlds without being reduced to them, signifying without being signified. Yet, we have not discovered how exactly we ascend to these essences, and the ways in which art reveals them. Towards this end, Deleuze makes the existential observation that despite their various worlds, works of art bear certain "family resemblances",[22] their qualities overlapping from one world to the next. These resemblances constitute what Deleuze calls a "style":

> Style is not the man, style is essence itself.
> Essence is not only particular, individual, but individualizing. Essence individualizes and determines the substances in which it is incarnated, like the objects it encloses within the rings of style: thus Vinteuil's reddening septet and white sonata, or the splendid diversity within Wagner's work. This is because essence is in itself difference. But it does not have the power to diversify, and to diversify itself, without also having the power to repeat itself, identical to itself. What can one do with essence, which is ultimate difference, except to repeat it, since it is irreplaceable and since nothing can be substituted for it? This is why great music can only be played again, a poem learned by heart and recited. Difference and repetition are only apparently in opposition. There is no great artist who dos no make us say: "The same and yet different."
> This is because difference, as the quality of a world, is affirmed only through a kind of autorepetition which transverses the various media and reunites different objects; repetition constitutes the degrees of an original difference, but also diversity constitutes the levels of a repetition no less fundamental. About the work of a great artist, we say: it's the same thing, on a different level. But we also say: it's different, but to the same degree. Actually, difference and repetition are the two inseparable and correlative powers of essence (48).

Those of us familiar with Deleuze recognize that this passage is a precursor to *Difference and Repetition*. There, he works out the

---

[22] The concept of "family resemblances" is Wittgenstein's (Wittgenstein 1960: 17).

details of the synonymy of difference and repetition at the ontological level. Nevertheless, in this passage he lays the groundwork of his future argument, enough so that we can identify several characteristics of the artistic essence.

Not only do works of art affect us and produce new signs and understandings in us, but we know from experience that different works of art affect us differently. As Proust's narrator shows us, we do not listen to Vinteuil, Wagner, or to any great artist in the same way, for they produce entirely different feelings, sensations, and impressions upon us. If an artist is said to have a particular 'style' it can only be because of the ability of their multiple artistic works to produce similar affects on us, over and over again, despite how we have changed. The 'family resemblances' between their works are resemblances of affect, repetitions of signs and understandings from each to each.

In this way, the artistic essence is not really identified so much by the artistic work or the artistic act, but by the similar signs and common qualities they engender. If we can speak of a 'Wagnerian' style, or a 'Baroque', 'Gothic', 'Surreal', or any other type of style, these abstract terms correlate to a plethora of different qualities and procedures, that although understood by these terms, are understood only vaguely and in an extremely abstract sense. Common qualities are identified and different materials correlated to them, though these series are forever changing, multiplying and dividing as we search the work of art and discover its infinite applications.

A style is composed not only in a multiplicity of artistic works and acts, but also multiple significations and significant worlds. We conceptualize it not as something which is understood, as much as it is a matrix of understandings. The style encompasses a collection of common qualities, which appear as signs and explode in multiple series, subjective understandings, and worlds:

> Style is the explication of the signs, at different rates of envelopment, following the associative chains proper to each of them, gaining in each case the breaking point of essence as Viewpoint... (147).

Every 'Viewpoint' is *a* world, a gathering of subjective series into a comprehensive perspective of *the world*. Style becomes a world the moment we begin to understand its common qualities and signs, interpreting their relations to the world, seizing upon the work of art's effect and applying it to our own knowledge. We delve into a work of art, not to realize it through itself (we already know its object!), but to realize it as essence, as a particular viewpoint or style that passes from one world to the next.

Therefore, every work of art repeats at least two effects. First, as the work of art opens our understanding back into materiality, it has the effect of producing new signs. A true artistic piece is infinite in terms of the signs it is able to affect us with. The test of art lies in our search of it. Quite simply, the more we search it, the more signs we find. Secondly, the work of art unites different semiotic worlds, such that its common qualities act as a matrix of these worlds and series of understanding. In the presence of art, our previous understandings are shattered, as we are led into new worlds and adapt to them. This effect repeats every time we consider the work of art, for genuine art never fails to produce new understandings, no matter how many times we return to it.

Inasmuch as art affects our understandings of the world, and leads us into new worlds, art splinters us from ourselves, dividing our intellect and identity into different orders. Art brings us to the threshold of all worlds, where all materials emerge as signs, and where all meanings and significations are simultaneous and infinite. Art touches upon materiality and upon the essences therein, such that it becomes an expression of "pure thought" (54), or the ideal effects of materiality: pure semiosis, before all semiotics. "[B]eyond the object, beyond the subject himself", art leads us to an immaterial and amorphous becoming of both (49).

The Virtual and the Two Kinds of Memories

The question remains, though, where this realm of pure semiosis resides ontologically. Proust himself offers an answer to this question, as he reflects upon Bergson's theory of memory. Deleuze interjects here and completes the argument that occurs between them:

> That the past does not have to preserve itself in anything but itself, because it is in itself, survives and preserves itself in itself-such are the famous theses of *Matter and Memory*. This being the past in itself is what Bergson called the virtual. Similarly in Proust, when he speaks of states induced by the signs of memory: "Real without being present, ideal without being abstract." It is true that, starting from this point, the problem is not the same in Proust and in Bergson, it is enough for Bergson to know that the past is preserved in itself... While Proust's problem is, indeed: how to save for ourselves the past as it is preserved in itself, as it survives in itself?... Let us note Proust's reaction: "We all possess our memories, if not the faculty of recalling them, the great Norwegian philosopher says according to M. Bergson... But what is a memory which one does not recall?" (57-58).

According to Bergson, voluntary memory is an expression of the pure past, which is preserved in-itself and functions independently from its memory images (Bergson 1991: 133). Memory images are the distinct and material expressions of the pure past, representing it as particular actions/thoughts. The same pure memory affects us with different memory images depending on the circumstances in which it is recalled, as these voluntary memories vary according to our reasons for soliciting them and the context in which they are remembered. Meanwhile, a pure memory resides immaterially and subconsciously within us, remaining 'real without being present'. 'Real' because they determine our concrete memories, but 'not present' because the actual past has past and the origins of these images no longer exist. Concrete memory is therefore composed of *signs* of the pure past, which signify its presence, without making it absolutely signified (Deleuze 1972: 58-63).

Immediately, we can see that Deleuze considers pure memories as essences, especially insofar as they affect us and become concrete images (objects and significances) for our consideration. Every pure memory is therefore an ideal essence that corresponds to some original moment in the past, wherein its productive value was inscribed into pure memory. Our memories are entirely artistic in this sense, expressing various material affections and signs, without any of them corresponding exactly with their immaterial essences. They are 'ideal without being abstract', understood through their affects, but without being completely signified by any of these understandings, as we understand them holistically, but never absolutely.

In addition to these voluntary memories (i.e. memory images), Proust exceeds Bergson in his concern for 'involuntary' memory:

> Involuntary memory seems to be based first of all upon the resemblance between two sensations, between two moments. But, more profoundly, the resemblance refers us to a strict *identity* of a quality common to the two sensations, or of a sensation common to the two moments, the present and the past. Thus the flavor [i.e. of the narrator's madeleine]: it seems that it contains a volume of duration which extends it through two moments at once. But, in its turn, the sensation, the identical quality, implies a relation with something *different* (58).

Memory images are material *signs* insofar as they represent the pure past without disclosing it exactly. This is the nature of the pure past – it is forgotten, and cannot be returned to, but it continues to affect us presently as signs and their affects.

This means that memories, whether voluntary or involuntary, are never objective signs, as they signify origins that belong to the immaterial past. Every memory image is therefore a sign of love, its origins lost in the past. But memories find their meaning in the present, and in the present circumstances which lead us voluntarily or involuntarily to recall them. Thus, they immediately signify their present affects, while simultaneously signifying a forgotten past. Hence their 'two moments at once': the memory image unites two worlds, one before us, the other behind us in the past, and for that reason all memories are ultimately concrete qualities of these two worlds and their series of understanding. Meanwhile, the essence of this quality stretches between these two series of time and significance, identical to both of them, but different in each.

Deleuze argues that voluntary signs of memory actually differ in kind from involuntary ones. The voluntary memory is immediately understood, belonging to a memory image that is given a place inside a series of present understanding. Most often these voluntary memories are signs of love, their past origins irrelevant to their present significance. However, they can also be qualities of multiple understandings, as the memory image is understood in multiple senses, multiple worlds.

In contrast, involuntary memories appear suddenly and violently, appearing on the spot so to speak, emerging without any specific sense. Concomitantly, they signify present worlds and past ones, eliciting a search that takes the memory as a quality of both:

> the resemblance between the two moments is transcended in
> the direction of a more profound identity, the contiguity which
> belonged to the past moment is transcended in the direction of
> a more profound difference... *The essential thing in*
> *involuntary memory is not resemblance, nor even identity,*
> *which are merely conditions, but the internalized difference,*
> *which becomes immanent* (58-59).

Unlike voluntary memory (where the past is recalled within present understandings, and towards understanding those series better), involuntary memory assaults *all* our present worlds and understandings with an actual repetition of a feeling or sensation first discovered in the past. All at once its sign expresses an internalized difference that becomes an infinity of associations, as the memory defies our understandings, recalling something more profound. Deleuze recognizes at once that:

> This ideal reality, this *virtuality* [my emphasis], is essence,
> which is realized or incarnated in involuntary memory. Here as
> in art, envelopment or involution, remains the superior state of
> essence. And involuntary memory retains its two powers: the
> difference in the past moment, the repetition in the present one.
> But essence is realized in involuntary memory to a lesser
> degree than in art, it is incarnated in a more opaque matter.
> First of all, essence no longer appears as the ultimate quality of
> a singular viewpoint, as did artistic essence, which was
> individual and even individualizing. Doubtless it is particular,
> but it is a principle of localization rather than of

individuation... But, from another viewpoint, it is already general, because it grants this revelation in a sensation "common" to two places, to two moments. In art too, the quality of essence was expressed as a quality common to two objects; but the artistic essence thereby lost nothing of its singularity, was not alienated, because the two objects and their relation were entirely determined by the point of view of essence, without any margin of contingence. This is no longer the case with regard to involuntary memory: essence begins to assume a minimum of generality. Which is why Proust says that the sensuous signs already refer to a "general essence," like the signs of love or the worldly signs (60).

'*Virtuality*' is Deleuze's preferred term (borrowed from Bergson) for the realm of ideal essences. Out of the virtuality of the past (i.e. the essences of past events), we get voluntary and involuntary memories. These are both signs, but only insofar as they are searched. In contrast to voluntary memories, involuntary ones offer us a glimpse of the pure past, which exists virtually in the essence of a past event. But unlike the signs of art, this essence is somewhat diluted, all too easily falling back into significant representations, like present objects and memory images. Correlated to these, whatever pure essences and productive and artistic powers these involuntary memories represent are blocked by these objective and subjective representations. Instead of revealing the multiplicity of these essences, and becoming signs of art, these involuntary memories are instead associated with present objects, and therefore go no further than sensuous signs. In this way, each memory takes on a qualitative character, expressed by a particular feeling or mood that generalizes a group of objects, images, and significations.

Past events and past essences determine the material signs of memory, but these are entirely infinite in that all material signs belong to them simply because what has past in them has become present in us. Existentially and ontologically, all signs are signs of an involuntary memory, of an essence that has touched us virtually, but which is presently expressed in our material experience of it. And so, despite our tendency to treat involuntary memories qualitatively, they are ultimately signs of art, which have no definite qualities, only more or less proximate ones. Our search of the past boarders on art, and has its source entirely in it, but this is only ever expressed before us materially, in the art and act of living and understanding presently.

However, it is only by an extreme effort that we can sustain this production of the past and the search of involuntary memory. Proust himself is a case in point: chasing the essence of his past, he produced a magnificent work of art that spanned most of his life and brought him to the edge of both his sanity and health. Proust's art and Proust's essence were his own involuntary memories, which were expressed in a completely manifold way by all the worlds of all his 'place-names' (Combray, Balbec, Swann, Guermantes, etc.). The search for lost time begins time anew in every viewpoint generated by these place-names, which signify completely different worlds from the narrator's past. Thus, in Proust, all places and names correspond to essences which are not so much in the past, as much as they create 'pasts'.

As infinite, all essences are pre-significant and therefore pre-temporal (at least in any sense that could be understood). They populate virtuality simultaneously, dynamically revolving around each other so as to express a pure time wherein all significant temporalities are simultaneous to each other. Insofar as signs convey these essences, signs are equally a-temporal and infinite. It is only after they have been understood that they are given temporal sense, signified in time's objects and measures (e.g. clocks, timers, cycles of days, etc).

Virtuality and Essences

The virtual is real, but only inasmuch as it is expressed in matter.[23] This means that essences do not exist apart from the materials they form. Materials and signs do not emanate from essences, but are within them. Essences are not transcendental, and do not issue materials from outside materiality, but from within it. In Deleuze's material realism, there is no 'outside', no metaphysical or transcendental influence on materiality.[24]

---

[23] A more detailed account of Bergson's virtual and its relation to materiality is to be found in Deleuze's book *Bergsonism*, which contains the argument in full (Deleuze 1991).

[24] Rather, "metaphysics, and with it the world as we perceive it, has reached its end, is therefore not a proposition in the philosophy of culture, but an expression

Both the diversity of these materials and the complexity of their relations attest to the dynamism of their essences. They express profound virtual relations between them, wherein essences relate to other essences, compounding their powers so as to create different effects. The essences of materiality are completely dynamic, this dynamism expressed in turn as concrete and individuated effects and materials. *Essences are therefore always* immanent, *not* transcendent, *inhering within materiality as that which ideally differentiates its infinite monism into particular materials.*[25]

When Deleuze declares that essences are "ideal without being abstract" (57), he affirms that although essences are without absolute form, they are not 'abstract' because they *are* their concrete productions. In contrast, abstraction always implies some degree of transcendence, whether it be of an object or series of objects signifying another (abstract knowledge), or of some ideal form emanating into matter while remaining distinct from it (e.g. Plato's "forms", or Plotinus' "One")*.*[26] But this is not the case here. Instead, Deleuze's ideal 'forms' have no 'form' to speak of, and are more like powers of self-organization, inhering within materiality so as to become an infinity of formed matters without corresponding to them, or transcending them.

In this way, every essence is always expressed in two different ways, and at two different levels. On the one hand, it represents ideal essences and powers that are entirely virtual, inhering within matter and inscribing forms in it. On the other hand, there is the material expression that they actually form, the concrete modes of materiality that correspond exactly to virtual limits. Every essence signifies both a virtual ideal and actual affects. As the former produces the latter, it remains virtual, expressed concretely as a world and as understandings of that world, without itself being concretely understood:

> Essence, according to Proust, as we have tried to show above,
> is not something seen, but a kind of superior *viewpoint*, an

---

of the state of our being We are ourselves the proof of that death of metaphysics (Schirmacher 1984: 603-609)." For Schirmacher, as for Deleuze, our existential reality proves the futility of metaphysics.

[25] See Chapter V for Deleuze's complete argument.

[26] See Plato's *Republic*, and Plotinus' *Enneads*.

> irreducible viewpoint which signifies at once the birth of the world and the original character of a world. It is in this sense that the work of art always constitutes and reconstitutes the beginning of the world, but also forms a specific world absolutely different from the others, and envelops a landscape or immaterial site quite distinct from the site where we have grasped it (98).

Essences are the building blocks of all worlds, the eternal differences that characterize individual worlds, works of art, and other infinite searches.

More like a 'superior viewpoint', an essence coordinates a world without being signified by any particular part of it. Our search of any sign is our attempt to try to attain this 'superior viewpoint', and to grasp the essence in its entirety. Instead of reaching it though, we grasp only its creative power, building that world and relating it to a multiplicity of others. As these other worlds correspond to their own essences, our search virtually corresponds to the relation of all essences to each other, the infinite production of signs and meanings, or the simultaneity of all worlds. *As the virtual reside of all essences, materiality therefore infinitely and absolutely represents all possible worlds.*[27]

As differentiating and differentiated, the essences of materiality enjoy a certain "transversality", which is Deleuze's term (borrowed from Proust) for any phenomena "which has the power to be the whole *of* these parts without totalizing them, the unity *of* these parts without unifying them" (150).[28] We have already seen how both materiality and its essences are transversal, and how it is impossible to signify them. Essences and their expressions, the virtual and the concrete, are bound together in a single material realism, a 'materiality'. However, we have no way of understanding this unity significantly. Significance exists at a different ontological level than the virtual essences, whose immaterial relations precede and posit significant bonds.

In the *Search:*

---

[27] That is to say concretely, not metaphysically, as in Leibniz (Leibniz 1991: 68-81).
[28] The concept is not only Proustian, but Spinozist, as we will see in Chapter V.

> It is transversality which constitutes the singular unity and
> totality of the Méséglise Way and of the Guermantes Way,
> without suppressing their difference or distance: "between these
> routes certain transversals were established" (149).

In this particular case, the unifying quality belongs to the
narrator's childhood home, the front door of which leads down
the Méséglise Way, the back door of which opens onto the
Guermantes Way. Meanwhile, the house represents not only the
shared quality of these two worlds, but an essence that relates
these two worlds, which in turn have their own respective
essences. The transversality of the narrator's childhood home,
both in its concrete quality and in its ideal essence, shows us
how one essence or world can unite multiple essences and
multiple worlds all at once in a 'singular unity and totality' that
nonetheless preserves them in their differences.

The whole of Proust's *Search* proceeds in this way, as
the semiotic series of places, names, people, and events resonate
together in this masterwork of art. All these exchanges represent
"transversality, which proceeds from one sentence to another in
[Proust's] book, and which even unites Proust's book to those he
preferred, by Nerval, Chateaubriand, Balzac" (150). The *Search*
explodes into other searches (Balzac's, Chateubriand's, Nerval's,
etc.), as Proust's art is infinitely bound to those he has been
inspired by.

In all cases, transversality is the tendency for any single
essence to implicate a multiplicity, for all multiplicies to
express a single essence, or for all essences to express a single
material unity. The diversity of the parts is never totalized, never
captured by some ideal signification or meaning, but instead
incorporated within an ideal essence that infinitely differentiates
itself from itself in its relation to other essences:

> Beyond designated objects, beyond intelligible and formulated
> truths, but also beyond subjective chains of association and
> resurrections by resemblance or contiguity, are the essences
> which are alogical or supralogical. They transcend the states of
> subjectivity no less than the properties of the object. It is the
> essence which constitutes the sign insofar as it is irreducible to
> the object emitting it; it is the essence which constitutes the

> meaning insofar as it is irreducible to the subject apprehending it (46).

The essences are '*alogical*' because they constitute the very meanings that are logically understood.[29] Thus, their insignificance makes them pre-logical, instantiating all logical series. However, the essences are never *il*logical, for illogic can only be judged *a posteriori* to the constitution of a logical series, namely as that which is excluded from that series (i.e. that which contradicts it). Essences are on a completely different ontological and epistemological level than 'illogic', which is always concretely expressed into semiological orders. As virtual, and constitutive of these, all essences are thus multi-logical or *supralogical*, asserting an infinite multiplicity of logics simultaneously.

Furthermore, essences constitute subjects, creating the very meanings and identities that are then grouped into subjective series of understanding:

> It is essence which constitutes subjectivity. It is not the individuals who constitute the world, but the worlds enveloped, the essences which constitute the individuals... Essence is not only individual, it *individualizes* (43).

An essence always has a double effect, constituting individual signs and objects, and then grouping these signs and objects into different series. Insofar as these series preserve their meanings from each other, they become different subjective viewpoints. As every person experiences and participates in multiple worlds, they have multiple subjectivities at their disposal, different identities that they can assume, or different viewpoints through which they can interpret the world.

---

[29] The meaning of the subject expresses its own logic in turn, representing various conservations of meaning (codes) and necessary limits to their relations, which individualize them. A subject or logic can only function through the association of specific objects through significant codes, rules and laws. But the subjective logic is defined not so much by what it includes, but by what it excludes, namely all that its rules and codes do not allow (i.e. contradictions, infinite meanings, irrational variables, etc.). Every signification, subject, or logic is achieved only by excluding certain essences and their materials in favour of others.

As we embrace essences, they become particular subjective world-views through our understandings of them. Each world-view is nonetheless in the midst of all the other essences and world-views that we embody, adapting and changing according to them. In this dynamism, we likewise embody their multiple worlds, viewpoints, and styles, so that virtually we are properly schizophrenic and multi-personal, our identity changing according to the most dominant essences within us. To touch upon an essence is therefore to participate in this schizophrenia, and to embrace the essences' abundance of subjective views, mixing them with our own, in a reconstitution of them all.

Yet, how do we touch upon essences? We have already seen how they are revealed though qualities, styles, and works of art, and Deleuze has even insinuated that the latter embody their infinite expression, and manifest it within us:

> But precisely how is essence incarnated in the work of art? Or, what comes down to the same thing, how does an artist-subject manage to "communicate" the essence which individualizes him and makes him eternal? It is incarnated in substances. But these substances are ductile, so kneaded and refined that they become entirely spiritual...free substances which are expressed equally well through words, sounds, and colors....At the same time that essence is incarnated in a substance, the ultimate quality constituting it is therefore expressed as the *quality common* to two different objects, need in this luminous substance, plunged into this refracting medium. It is in this that style consists...Which is to say that style is essentially metaphor. But metaphor is essentially metamorphosis, and indicates how the two objects exchange their determinations, exchange even the names which designate them, in the new medium which confers the common quality upon both of them (46-47).

The 'substances' are those various materials in which the essence incarnates itself. These materials may be 'words, sounds, colours, etc.', as well as signs, significations, and their various relations, as we have seen. However, the more any one of these is searched, the more 'ductile' they become, signifying multiple objects and series simultaneously, and drawing us into increasingly diverse worlds. They become an increasingly 'spiritual' signs, signs of art or of the pure production of an essence which can manifest itself anywhere, but always to a different effect, in a complete schizophrenia of meaning. At their concrete limit, signs act as the *common qualities* of an infinity of orders. And insofar as these common qualities are inherent to an infinity of orders, they necessarily embody essences, the true infinites.[30]

Although individualized differently in every world of which they are a part, the search of a common quality brings these meanings together, exchanging them as though they are metaphors of each other. In effect, the common quality hybridizes objects and worlds, as these understandings are blended. Meanwhile, new instances of the quality are also found, its essence repeats its power of differentiation and difference, germinating new objects and new series of understanding for them.

When Deleuze identifies the common qualities as 'spiritual', we must understand that by 'spiritual' he ontologically means nothing different than the 'virtual' that we have discussed. The term is used, however, to emphasize the dynamic sense of the virtual, whose essences infinitely relate so as to produce and animate concrete matter in turn. The spirituality of Deleuze is not metaphysical, nor transcendent, but virtual and immanent. Essences are 'free substances' in that they are concretely manifested, but in infinite expressions. An essence (i.e. a 'spirit') inheres in all of these simultaneously, haunting them by continually relating them to each other, compounding them and refracting them in new metaphors and artistic creations:

> Essence is always an artistic essence. But once discovered, it is incarnated not only in spiritualized substances, in the immaterial signs of the work of art, but also in other realms, which will hence forth be integrated into the work of art. It passes then into media which are more opaque, into signs which are more material. It loses there certain of its original characteristics, assumes others which express the descent of essence into these increasingly rebellious substances (50).

---

[30] See Mauss' book *The Gift* for more on the 'spiritual' nature of exchange, and how the spiritual significance of language and understanding is equally embodied by the exchange of goods (Mauss, 8-18).

The primary substance of materiality is a multiplicity of 'spiritualized substances', dynamic intensities and forces (i.e. essences) which are expressed transversally into the multiplicity of material signs, objects, and significations. If the essences are spiritualized, it is because they are expressed dynamically, incarnated and animated in materials, while remaining virtual and invisible. Like an exceptional 'poltergeist', materiality not only moves, creates, and relates essences, but also expresses them in equally dynamic concrete substances. The spirit of substance is always dual: generative and productive.[31]

Meanwhile, the various materials produced out of an essence are hierarchized in terms of the degree to which they express this artistic essence and its power. The primary expressions of essence are signs, and of signs, qualities express essence most clearly, demonstrating their common and infinite nature. The signs of love follow after these, revealing the multiple worlds of essences, as well as their multifarious senses. Lastly, the worldly signs demonstrate the essential powers that generate objects and create the basic meanings of understanding and intelligence.

Worldly signs are the most 'opaque' signs, being the 'more material' of the three concrete types and having no meaning outside of their objects. The signs of love are only a little less opaque. Their origins are unknown, which allows them to vary their meaning depending on the material situation in which they are found. While 'qualities' approach the immaterial because of their transversality. Although they adhere to specific materials and series of understanding, they compound these infinitely and circulate among infinite senses.

Only these sensuous signs retain the 'spiritualized' nature of essences, straddling multiple series without having an absolute sense. Were they to have one, we would still be no closer to accounting for the diversity of all the others they relate to. Rather, the question would remain, 'By what difference do all these series have their difference?', that is to say, 'What causes their differences to each other?' Only an invisible essence can

---

[31] Likewise, we find this distinction in Spinoza (Book I, prop. 33, schol. 2), namely between *natura naturata* and *natura naturans* (Spinoza: 54-56).

account for this primordial difference, positing them without rendering itself finite. Qualities reveal the essences, but only negatively, their infinite meaning betraying the even more profound production of meaning, which is infinitely meaningless.

Essences as Virtual Machines

Insofar as art produces meaning, art functions like a 'machine', slicing up sense in order to recompose it into a different world-view:

> The modern work of art is anything it may seem; it is even its very property of being whatever we like, of having the overdetermination of whatever we like, from the moment *it works*: the modern work of art is a machine an functions such... [The modern work of art is] machine and machinery whose meaning (anything you like) depends solely on its functioning, which, in turn, depends on its separate parts. The modern work of art has no problem of meaning, it has only a problem of use.
>
> Why a machine? Because the work of art, so understood, is essentially productive - productive of certain truths. No one has insisted more than Proust on the following point: that the truth is produced, that it is produced by orders of machines which function within us, that it is extracted from our impressions, hewn out of our life, delivered in a work (128-129).

We 'use' the modern work of art every time we search it, allowing its virtual essence to affect us and modify our understanding. We 'extract' this machine by searching the common qualities found in the work of art, whose infinite significance becomes infinite affects within us.

The first 'truth' produced by the work of art, through its essence, are the new impressions it gives us, the new sensations it fills us with:

> All production starts from the impression, because only the impression unites in itself the accident of the encounter and the necessity of the effect, a violence which it obliges us to

> undergo. Thus all production starts from a sign, and supposes
> the depth and darkness of the involuntary (130).

Essence has an effect, namely the 'involuntary' and 'insignificant' production of impressions and their existential importance to us. Materiality delivers a sign over to us, which seizes us 'violently', conjuring other sensations and feelings that demand we understand it. The first truth of a work of art is therefore a search, which is likewise the first truth of all signs.

The essence of the work of art, meanwhile, resides between the signs and impression we are affected with. Like an invisible third-party, it scrambles our thoughts and actions, each time creating new meanings for them, in different combinations of impressions:

> Meaning itself is identified with this development of the sign,
> as the sign was identified with the involution of meaning. So
> that Essence is finally the third term which dominates the other
> two, which presides over their movement: essence complicates
> the sign and the meaning, it holds them *in complication*, it puts
> the one in the other...like the sufficient reason for the other
> two terms and for their relation (89).

An engagement with essence 'complicates' meaning by producing new signs and new material relations between our impressions. The more an essence's signs are searched, the more meanings are found for it, complicating its objects and their significance. This is because "[i]t is essence which, in each case, determine[s] the relation between sign and meaning. This relation [i]s all the closer when essence [i]s incarnated with more necessity and individuality; all the looser, on the contrary, when essence assume[s] a greater generality and [i]s incarnated in more contingent data" (88). The meaning of a sign is undone by the essence of that sign, which bears in itself an infinity of meanings. So long as we search a sign or its meanings, we communicate with this essence, and are under its influence.

Essence as Truth and Violence

    Proust and Signs begins with the assertion that "the Search is not simply an effort of recall, an exploration of memory: search, *recherché*, is to be taken in the strong sense of the term, as we say "the search for truth"" (3). We need to now explicate what Deleuze's overall concept of truth is, how it is revealed by searching and what its overall relation is to both signs and essences.

    We begin with a sign. This sign disrupts us existentially, prompting a search for its meaning. Deleuze identifies this 'disruption' as a type of violence:

> There is always the violence of a sign which forces us into the search, which robs us of peace. The truth is not to be found by affinity, nor by good will, but is *betrayed* by involuntary signs (16).

The sign and the existential disturbance we feel along side it express the search in us. These are involuntary, insofar as we cannot help but receive signs from the world and be existentially poised towards them in this way. They express a virtual essence, our contact with which produces these affects on us, as if we were possessed by a spirit:

> We search for truth only when we are determined to do so in terms of a concrete situation, when we undergo a kind of violence which impels us to such a search. Who searches for truth? The jealous man, under the pressure of the beloved's lies. There is always the violence of a sign which forces us into the search, which robs us of peace. The truth is not to be found by affinity, nor by good will, but is *betrayed* by involuntary signs (15-16).

The essence of the sign is expressed both as the concrete sign and its disturbance, which prompts the concrete search for its meaning among the other materials before us. Signs are entirely violent; not only by the disturbance they elicit within us, but because they force us out of our subjective knowledge, out of the lies of our understanding, into new worlds. Everything we believe we know is disrupted, and the cohesion of our 'self' (which is only so many series of understandings) is ripped apart:

> There are few themes on which Proust insists as much as on this one: truth is never the product of a prior disposition but the result of a violence in thought. The explicit and conventional significations are never profound; the only profound meaning is the one which is enveloped, implicated in an external sign... Truth depends on an encounter with something which forces us to think, and to seek truth...Precisely it is the sign which constitutes the object of an encounter, and which works this violence upon us (16).

If the meaning of the sign is profound, it is because it has no necessary meaning. It is between meanings and therefore implicates a 'profound' number of series and understandings. If we do not find a meaning for it, or forget it altogether in the materiality of the world, then we are faced with this profundity, this schizophrenia of multiple series and the violence that the sign does upon each of them.

The sign is unnerving because it stimulates sensation while at the same time it stubbornly avoids sense. It necessitates a break in the series of our understanding, wreaking its violence on all the series, infinitely signifying beyond them. In order to accommodate it, we are forced to change the order of our understanding until it has its place and is given a corresponding meaning. Unless this meaning is found for it, its violence continues unabated, existentially disturbing us and preoccupying all our actions and thoughts.

Signs therefore compel us to signify their 'truth', that is, to signify their essence and virtuality. We interpret them according to the objects and materials that surround them, extending their meaning through these in order to discover their essential truth and reality. However, this essential truth and reality is virtual and infinite, rendered in the concrete but impossible to signify with the concrete. In this way, the infinite and virtual truth of essence becomes the concrete meaninglessness of the sign, the fleetingness of its significance in the face of its infinite search.

Ironically then, the more we understand about a sign, the further we are from its truth. We extend our worlds and series of understanding only at the expense of giving up our search, limiting the sign's infinite productive power to the rules and constraints of our understandings. Those who boast of 'intelligence' boast no more than the ability to conquer several of these complex series, milking logical consequences out of the series at their disposal. They have a broad understanding, but this is not the same as saying they are capable of 'thinking'. They inscribe complex networks of significations, and yet the more they do, the less they are actually involved in thought.

There is a certain law of conservation of meaning at work within intelligence, wherein the series of understanding retain their differences from each other by adhering to exclusive codes of meaning. Intelligence would therefore be the ability to repeatedly translate these series into one another, while at the same time strictly adhering to their separate codes. Intelligence extracts the logical consequences of our understandings, building new ones between them, and extending our previous. If the intelligent man appears profound, it is because they can manage so many series at once, preserving their objectivity as they go.

However, intelligence signifies a profound ignorance of essence and the world. As it is confined to its finite series, it fails to arrive at the infinite. The intelligent abound in abstract knowledge only by becoming insensitive to the world around them. They fail to realize the infinite potential of every sign and material, instead proceeding as if all signs and impressions were exclusively and finitely organized, to and with each other. An intelligent person understands much, but thinks nothing, for they produce nothing new in thought. They have many facts, but no truth, no intuition of essences or of the infinite worlds outside their own.

The search opposes intelligence, insofar as it opens itself up to truth and the creation of new signs and new significations. At the level of intelligence, everything is signified and re-signified, in orders of understanding that can only abstract each other and not expand upon the fundamental signs and meanings at their basis:

> In the language of signs, on the contrary, there is no truth
> except in what is done in order to deceive, in the meanders of

> what conceals the truth, in the fragments of a deception and a disaster: there is no truth except a betrayed truth, that which is both surrendered by the enemy, and revealed by oblique views or by fragments... When a part is valid for itself, when a fragment speaks in itself, when a sign appears, it may be in two very different fashions: either because it permits us to divine the whole from which it is taken, to reconstitute the organism or the stature to which it belongs, and to seek out the other part which belongs to it- or else, on the contrary, because there is no other part which corresponds to it, no totality into which it can enter, no unity from which it is torn and to which it can be restored (100).

The 'truth' of the sign's essence is this 'oblique' and 'fragmented' view, facilitated by a sign. It presents two choices. First, we can compound these fragments, correlating them to each other and surrendering them over to consistent and significant meanings. In this case, we totalize the meaning of the essence, abstracting it concretely in series of understanding and intelligence. Or secondly, we can complicate these fragments by realizing they do not signify absolutely, but instead diverge into an infinite number of series, irreconcilable on that account. The essence is expressed, and even meaningful, but in no ways uniformly or sufficiently. Instead, the networks of intelligence collapse in the overwhelming diversity of so many new and confused impressions.

This confusion is what allows us to eternally return to the process of thinking and building intelligence anew:

> Truth depends on an encounter with something which forces us to think, and to seek the truth. The accident of encounters, the pressure of constraints are Proust's two fundamental themes. Precisely, it is the sign which constitutes the object of an encounter, and which works this violence upon us (16).

Without the aggravation and frustration this produces, we would have no reason to search, and therefore no impetus to build knowledge in the first place, for:

> Who would seek the truth if he had not first leaned that a gesture, an intonation, a greeting must be interpreted? Who would seek the truth if he had not first suffered the agonies

> inflicted by the beloved's lies? The ideas of the intelligence are often "surrogates" of disappointment. Pain forces the intelligence to seek, just as certain unaccustomed pleasures set memory in motion. It is the responsibility of the intelligence to understand, and to make us understand, that the most frivolous signs of worldliness refer to laws, that he most painful signs of love refer to repetitions. Then we learn ho to make us of other beings: frivolous or cruel, they have "posed before us," they are no longer anything but the incarnation of themes which transcend them, or the fragments of a divinity which is powerless against us. The discovery of the worldly laws gives a meaning to signs which remained insignificant, taken in isolation; but above all the comprehension of our amorous repetitions changes into joy each of those signs which taken in isolation gave us so much pain... Then, thanks to intelligence, we discover what we could not know at the start: that we were already apprenticed to signs when we supposed we were wasting our time... Time wasted, lost time − but also time regained, recovered time. To each kind of sign there doubtless corresponds a privileged line of time. The worldly signs imply chiefly a time wasted; the signs of love envelope especially a time lost. The sensuous signs often afford us the means of regaining time, restore it to us at the heart of times lost. The signs of art, finally give us a time regained, an original absolute time which includes all the others (23-24).

Relative to intelligence, the sign is a waste of time, for it has no definite place in the order of knowledge and its interpretation is insecure. Through the search though, the same sign redeems itself by implicating a whole conundrum of new significations, each one of which gives us the pleasure of knowing more about the world. If the worldly signs waste more of our time than the other material signs, it is because they can only result in objects that do nothing to signify themselves beyond a bare objectivity and consequently give us little joy because they add so little to our intelligence. The signs of love similarly waste our time, as they find their meaning in the knowledge we already possess and thus bring us no new joy when their meaning is finally unraveled. The sensuous signs, on the other hand, truly lead us into other worlds, where the same quality extends to entirely new meanings, entirely new joys. Finally, the signs of art are embraced, for they are expressed in infinite meanings that compound those worlds and multiply them even further, in limitless expressions and unbound pleasures. Deleuze's 'truth', therefore, inheres completely within matter as the eternal, infinite, and virtual essences that are expressed without limit in the concrete. We grasp them most closely in the signs of art, which produce endless meanings and significations without ever being adequately expressed by any of them. And so, Deleuze advises us that "in a world reduced to a multiplicity of chaos, it is only the formal structure of the work of art, insofar as it does not refer to anything else, which can serve as unity" (149). For Deleuze, art is the basis of truth and must be elevated to the highest level of human expression. Art's formal structure consists in the very truths and essences we seek in all our searches. Contrariwise, intelligence neither prompts this truth nor this art. Rather, art animates the intelligence, insofar as it creates and organizes the signs from which intelligence is wrought, including the pains that drive us to search, as well as the possibility of that search itself.

This truth "is not revealed, it is betrayed; it is not communicated, it is interpreted; it is not willed, it is involuntary" (160).[32] It announces itself at the end of our intelligence, as a sign that betrays the insufficiency of its meanings. Our knowledge reverts back into being a sign, this time a sign of itself and of its very limit. Beyond that limit lies the search and entirely new worlds that our intelligence has not accounted for. Voluntary intelligence can do no better than to exhaust itself in logical and abstract extensions until this limit is reached and a new sign emerges involuntarily. At the level of truth, signs are just signs to each other, not for each other. Hence their involuntary nature: no will or volition can be ascribed to them, because there are as of yet no subjects or bodies to claim them. The truth is precisely a breakdown of all subjectivity or objectivity. It is a turning away from the will into the chaos of the primary interpretation or re-interpretation that is sensation, thinking, and loving.

Accordingly, Deleuze can make a rather strong attack on the history of Philosophy itself:

---

[32] Furthermore, Deleuze goes on to say that "Voluntary thought gives us only possible truths", that is, particular objects and meanings (164).

> The mistake of Philosophy is to presuppose within us a benevolence of thought, a natural love of truth. Thus philosophy arrives at only abstract truths which compromise no one and do not disturb... They remain gratuitous, because they are born of the intelligence which accords them only a possibility, and not of a violence or of an encounter which would guarantee their authenticity. The ideas of the intelligence are valid only because of their explicit, hence conventional, signification. There are few themes on which Proust insists as much as on this one: truth is never the product of a prior disposition but the result of a violence in thought. The explicit and conventional significations are never profound; the only profound meaning is the one which is enveloped, implicated in an external sign (16).

We are not naturally disposed towards truth, rather truth affects us each time violently, forcing us out of our subjective intelligence, back into unfamiliar worlds. It is always easier to fall into the trap of intelligence, which 'gratuitously' has a place for everything and a signification for all its objects. Furthermore, most intelligence is borrowed from the languages, codes, and norms of society. We are taught within disciplines of thought, that each function according to their own narratives, logic, and grammars that amount to so many 'explicit and conventional significations'.[33] Intelligence finds fertile soil in the lot of 'established' human knowledge. For this reason, most of our subjective series are based in these institutional frameworks, as we relegate our severe experience of signs to the passive networks of common knowledge and logic. Intelligence becomes the ability to survey and regurgitate this knowledge without actually contributing new thoughts to its overarching domain. Instead of the violence of signs and genuine thought, we fall back on what everyone else thinks, trying the utmost to give all our signs a place there. This affords us instantaneous meaning and significance, and thus the shortest route to the pleasures of knowledge, though these joys are all too brief, for we continue to be assaulted by signs of love, qualities of other worlds, and art that refuses to take its place in the general order that we have

---

[33] We see here an early version of Deleuze's famous chapter "The Image of Thought", found in *Difference and Repetition* (Deleuze 1994: 129-167).

learned. Our jealousy builds as we realize that common knowledge is not enough to explain our love. Our confusion mounts, when qualities betray their definitions. And our frustration climaxes in expressions of art that scramble all the codes and lead us involuntarily into new worlds, however brief they may be.

Deleuze's condemnation of philosophy reveals his own frustration with the wisdom that its discipline claims, which has undoubtedly betrayed and failed him in so many ways. He even calls philosophy, "a voluntary and premeditated exercise of thought by which we may determine the order and content of objective significations" (29).

Against this, Deleuze asks us to embrace 'external signs' that "force us to think: no longer *recognizable* objects, but things which do violence, *encountered* signs" (166). Philosophy is for him a violence of thought that destroys significant orders, and expresses new and emerging meanings outside of what has been thought and signified hitherto. On account of this unfamiliarity and this unpredictability, philosophy is filled with entirely dangerous notions, which disrupt and rearrange everything we know:

> Each time we propose a concrete and dangerous thought, we know that it does not depend on an explicit decision or method, but on an encountered refracted violence which leads us in spite of ourselves to Essences. For the essences dwell in dark regions, not in the temperate zones of the clear and the distinct. They are involved in what forces us to think; they do not answer to our voluntary effort; they let themselves be conceived only if we are forced to do so (165).

Giving ourselves over to involuntary signs, we re-approach these essences so that new signs and significant values can be produced. For good or for bad, without this violence, without this dangerous "leap", we would never advance in our understanding of ourselves and our relation to the world (Schirmacher 1989: 125-134).[34] Without explicating signs, we

---

[34] "The leap without a net, the renunciation of substance, the ease of thought are metaphors of the artist's existence, foretold us by Friedrich Nietzsche in Zarathustra. What once only the mystics dared and what had to destroy them will become common practice in the technological world. Zarathustra's brothers and

remain victims of their hidden truth. Embracing them, we can at least come to approximate this truth and grow symbiotically with it.

For Deleuze, philosophy is utterly dangerous and brutal. Most importantly though, it does not begin with the pre-established knowledge of human science, nor with the history of philosophy itself, but with signs, with an involuntary attack from the abyss that overwhelms us and compels us to search. The path to philosophy is through 'Egyptology', and "we must be Egyptologists" (91), for:

> *There is no Logos, there are only hieroglyphs.* To think is therefore to interpret, is therefore to translate. The essences are at once the thing to be translated and the translation itself, the sign and the meaning. They are involved in the sign in order to force us to think, they develop in the meaning in order to be necessarily conceived. Everywhere is the hieroglyph, whose double symbol is the accident of the encounter and the necessity of thought: "fortuitous and inevitable" (167).

We do not understand an essence, but we 'translate' it into infinite meanings. Our searches convert essences into concrete expressions, while signs act as the untranslatable, the always foreign and abject materials whose meaning is utterly variable, and only contingently secured. At the end of his book on Proust, Deleuze encourages philosophers to become Egyptologists, because he knows that by searching signs we actually participate in the eternal essences and truths of the world.

---

sisters are the dancing technician, the joyful saint, the anarchic ethicist. They leave no stone standing, and so we finally begin to live as human beings."

CHAPTER IV

The "Seven Criteria"

Now that the ontology of the sign has been established, its types explicated, and the 'truth' of the sign revealed, Deleuze summarizes his entire Proustian system of signs into seven criteria. We shall go through them one at a time to completely expound upon their relation to his overall concept.

The First Criteria:
The Sign's Material

> 1. *The matter in which the sign is embodied.* These substances are more or less resistant and opaque, more or less dematerialized, more or less spiritualized. The worldly signs, though they function in a void, are only the more material for that. The signs of love are inseparable from the weight of a face, from the texture of a skin, from the width and color of a cheek: things which are spiritualized only when the beloved sleeps. The sensuous signs are still material qualities: above all odors and tastes. It is only in art that the sign becomes immaterial, at the same time that its meaning becomes spiritual (84).

The sign emerges from materiality (i.e. the world; substance). It affects us, both as an individual sensation/impression, and as an existential feeling that compels us to understand that sensation/impression. This sensation/impression is 'more or less resistant and opaque' to meaning (i.e. understanding; signification; correlation to other actions/thoughts). The worldly signs are the most 'material' because they implicate a specific action/thought that gives them a concrete and objective meaning. The feeling correlated to its sensation/impression becomes the minimum of meaning.

As James tells us:

> our supposed little feeling gives a *what;* and if other feelings should succeed which remembered the first, its *what* may stand out as subject or predicate of some piece of knowledge-about, or some judgment, perceiving relations between it and other *whats* which the other feelings may know. The hitherto dumb [impression/sensation] will then receive a name and be no longer speechless. But every name, as students of logic know, has its 'denotation'; and the denotation always means some reality or content, relationless *ab extra* or with its internal relations unanalyzed, like the [feeling] which our primitive sensation is supposed to know (James 1974: 211).

In correlating to each other, the feeling and the sensation/impression it denotes become a basic object, though what this object signifies remains external to this relation.

Contrariwise, the signs of love emerge from the actions/thoughts of our love, but do not objectify themselves in these. Instead, they take on a subjective meaning that correlates the action/thought of our love to an object, or series of objects, to which we are familiar. However, any sign may disassociate from its objective or subjective meaning and become a quality in itself, simply by an existential turn away from those objective and subjective meanings, towards a consideration of that sign in relation to all available knowledge (i.e. the sum total of all actions, thoughts, signs, and meanings). This sign becomes a quality and is 'spiritualized' (i.e. generalizable) in that it may circulate and find meaning in multiple objects and series.

Finally, the signs of art are virtual substances (i.e. virtual machines; effects; essences) that are immanent to matter, but remain entirely virtual (i.e. spiritual; immanent; ideal but not abstract). They express concretely all possible actions, thoughts, signs and significations necessarily, but are without sufficient expression in any one of them, or any series of them. The signs of art repeat their expression infinitely in all concrete materials.

The Second Criteria:
The Method of Interpretation

> 2. *The way in which something is emitted and apprehended as a sign, but also the consequent dangers of an interpretation which may be objectivist or subjectivist.* Each type of sign refers us to the object which emits it, but also to the subject who apprehends and interprets it. We believe at first that we must see and hear; or else, in love, that we must avow our love (pay homage to the object); or else that we must observe and describe the sensuous phenomenon; that we must work, must think in order to grasp significations and objective values. Disappointed, we fall back into the play of subjective associations. But for each kind of sign, these two moments of the apprenticeship have a rhythm and specific relations (Deleuze 1972: 84).

There are four ways of interpreting a sign, corresponding to the four types of signs. The sign can be referred to the object that emits it, creating an objective (and objectivist) interpretation that correlates the sign of that object to itself. Or, the sign can be referred to another object or series of objects that do not emit it. In this case, the sign takes on a completely subjective meaning, drawn from one's own familiar significations. In both of these cases, there is the 'danger' that signifying the sign we will refuse to see its 'truth', namely that it actually signifies a virtual essence that is expressed in infinite objects and subjective series. Hence, the third way to interpret a sign, which is to find that sign in multiple objects and therefore make a sensuous quality of it. The sign will then take on multiple objective meanings, in addition to the diversity of subjective interpretations associated with those different objects.

Yet, we are still only considering the sign concretely, and have not approached its true infinite significance. The sign refuses to be satisfied by any objective, subjective, or qualitative meaning, but can instead be infinitely interpreted. In order to do so, the interpreter must touch upon the essence of the sign and realize that it is related to an infinity of others. This realization is a completely intuitive process, expressed in the never-ending search of all signs, objects, and meanings and the perpetual dissatisfaction with their significance. The practitioner of this infinite search is like an obsessed 'Egyptologist', interpreting signs, but always beyond whatever they signify, looking for their still greater significance. This 'Egyptology' is what Deleuze envisions philosophy should be: a perpetual search for truth (i.e. essences in all their concrete virtual relations).

Towards this end, philosophers must pursue and be aware of all four types of signs and be able to interpret all signs according to them. The worldly signs must be 'seen and heard', that is, grasped as individual objects of sense and meaningful simply as those objects. The signs of love must be 'avowed', affirmed and interpreted according to what we already know, so that we can begin to give our beloved a place in our knowledge, and try to understand them. If these signs of love 'pay homage to the object', it is because they signify through the objects that we already know and extract their subjective meaning from these precursory objective meanings simply by arranging them in series with each other. But it is only when these same objects become sensuous signs (i.e. qualities) that we begin to observe them in multiple objects and multiple subjective series, thus producing a much broader knowledge of all our objects and loves. Lastly, we find the signs of art behind them all, when we 'work' and 'think' towards all these ends in order to grasp all signs objectively, subjectively, and qualitatively. In art, we allow for all the different senses of a sign so that a maximum of knowledge can be achieved, and the truth and productive power of the sign can reach its highest degree.

The Third Criteria:
The Sign's Emotion

> 3. *The effect of the sign upon us, the kind of emotion it produces.* Nervous exaltation is produced by the worldly signs; suffering and anguish by the signs of love; extraordinary joy by the sensuous signs (but in which anguish still appears as the subsisting contradiction of being and nothingness); pure joy by the signs of art (84-85).

The relations of essences to each other produce virtual effects that are then realized as our concrete affections (i.e. signs and impressions, the correlations of which become meaningful and significant). Existentially, the sign produces an emotional reaction that makes us suffer because we do not know its correlative meaning. This emotion compels us to search for its meaning, so that we can understand both the object that solicits it, as well as its broader subjective and qualitative significance.

First, when we consider the worldly sign and its object, the emotion we feel is a "nervous exaltation" (7). We are unnerved by the sign's presence and feel compelled to understand it so that we can know whether this sign threatens or compliments our existence. If we cannot attribute this nervousness to an object, we are filled with 'suffering and anguish', understanding the sign only obliquely in its relation to our other subjective understandings. Similarly, the signs of love afford us no joy, signifying unfamiliar and threatening worlds, and succeeding only in making us jealous of others' familiarity with them. In contrast, the sensuous signs give us objective instances of themselves everywhere. Each time they do, they fill us with joyful emotion, as we understand them in our various worlds, and as they extend these worlds for us. Though, every time we give them these objective and subjective meanings, we circumnavigate their more important essence and its infinite significance. The sensuous signs give us immediate joy, but they contain an inauspicious fate, eventually disappointing us when we realize that these objects have distracted us from the infinite expression that they are capable of. Instead, we experience pure joy only when in the presence of art, which is infinitely expressed by different signs, objects, and meanings.

The worldly signs make us nervous because they are the least understood signs. At most, they secure an objective meaning, which tells us nothing about that object's relations to both ourselves and the rest of the world. Anything could be immanent to the worldly sign, and thus our apprehension before it: we simply do not know what it could signify.

The signs of love, on the other hand, leave us feeling disappointed because the various significances we find for them repeatedly fail, dissolving back into threatening and unfamiliar worldly signs. Our nervousness and uncertainty returns, as we realize we do not really know our lover and that they could betray us at anytime.

The sensuous signs actually find stable significant meaning in the various actions/thoughts and series of understanding of which they are a quality. In turn, they bring us joy each time one of these is discovered, for through them we begin to understand the world and come to knowledge of it.

If the signs of art bring us 'pure joy', it is because we have opened ourselves up to an endless stream of meanings, a relentless quality that continues to abound in significance. The signs of art can never disappoint because they refuse the complete signification of the worldly signs and the signs of love, taking these meanings as qualities themselves so that they become the sensuous signs of other things. Implicating all possible worlds, they repeat their joy over and over again in new worlds, new signs, and new understandings of them all.

The Fourth Criteria: The Nature of the Sign's Meaning

> 4. *The nature of meaning, and the sign's relation to its meaning.* The worldly signs are empty, they take the place of action and thought, they try to stand for their meaning. The signs of love are deceptive: their meaning inheres in the contradiction of what they reveal and try to conceal. The sensuous signs are truthful, but in them subsist the opposition of survival and nothingness; and their meaning is still material, it resides elsewhere. However, to the degree that we achieve art, the relation of sign and meaning becomes close. Art is the splendid final unity of an immaterial sign and a spiritual meaning (85).

The worldly signs set up meaning in a void, as the sign implicates its original impression and nothing more. There is no abstraction here, no degree of understanding, only the most basic objective meaning. Instead, we must reach the signs of love in order for the sign to begin signifying and for it to extend from this original meaning into other meanings and objects. As these objects begin to correlate to each other, our understanding grows, however this understanding is also formed in a void, as the true origins and causes of all these objects are displaced by these significations.

Meanwhile, the sensuous signs abound in a multiplicity of objective and subjective meanings, which link them to various series simultaneously. These meanings exchange their significance through shared qualities, so that one series is always subsuming another and one meaning of the sign is gained only at the disappearance of another. This circulation of series and meanings misses their singular truth, which resides in their essential infinity.

Embracing art, we allow this infinity to be expressed through us freely and therefore instantiate the real significance of a sign, the simultaneity of all these series. Instead of trying to voluntarily signify the sign, we allow it to involuntarily produce through us. Taken over by the spirit of the sign's essence, new impressions are created and we no longer signify the sign so much as we embrace its effect on all significations, in an intuitive production which not only affects what the sign means, but all other signs and meanings too.

The Fifth Criteria:
The Sign's Faculty

> 5. *The principal faculty which explicates or interprets the sign, which develops its meaning.* This faculty is intelligence, in the case of the worldly signs; intelligence, too, but in another fashion, in the case of the signs of love (the effort of intelligence is no longer supported by an exaltation which must be calmed, but by the sufferings of sensibility which must be transmuted into joy). In the case of the sensuous signs, it is involuntary memory and imagination as the latter is generated by desire. In the case of the signs of art, pure thought as the faculty of essences becomes the interpreter (85).

When Deleuze says the worldly signs are intelligent but 'in another fashion', he means that they constitute a 'meaning', but one that is less than 'understanding' or 'knowing' that object. The union of the sign to its object is the basic building block of intelligence, yet for something to be understood it needs to implicate itself in terms other than these origins. A subjective series must be created, wherein additional impressions, signs and objects get associated with the worldly sign and widen its expression. The objects of consciousness then continue to abstract themselves to and from each other, building networks of differentiated subjective series that are each portions of intelligence. However, in order to bring more joy, one must keep expounding upon these subjective series and deliver them over into further significations of the world. New signs, actions, and thoughts must be extracted from worldliness so that truths may be established in different origins. The signs of love become qualities the moment we begin to look for different origins for them in the world. Yet, the arrival of these new origins is involuntary, given over from that worldliness and fulfilling the desire of this new search, though insignificantly with amorphous signs. Whether through involuntary memories or involuntary imaginations, materiality is an infinite supply of other origins for our sensuous signs. This involuntary production expresses an altogether different realm, a 'pure materiality' that simultaneously expresses an infinity of concrete images.

The Sixth Criteria:
The Sign's Temporality

> 6. *The temporal structures of the lines of time implicated in the sign, and the corresponding type of truth.* It always takes time to interpret a sign, all time is the time of an interpretation, that is, of a development. In the case of the worldly signs, we waste our time, for these signs are empty and we find them intact or identical at the end of their development. ...in love, the truth always comes too late. Love's time is a lost time because the sign develops only to the degree that the self which corresponded to its meaning disappears. The sensuous signs offer us a new structure of time: time rediscovered at the heart of lost time itself, an image of eternity. This is because the sensuous signs (unlike the signs of love) have the power either to awaken by desire and imagination, or to reawaken by involuntary memory, the Self that corresponds to their meaning. Lastly, the signs of art define time regained: an absolute primordial time, a veritable eternity which unites sign and meaning.
>
> Time wasted, time lost, time rediscovered, and time regained are the four lines of time. But we must note that if each type of sign has its particular line, it participates in the other lines as well, encroaches on them as it develops. *It is therefore on the lines of time that the signs intersect and*

multiply their combinations. Time wasted is extended in all the
other signs, except the signs of art. Conversely, time lost is
already present in the worldly signs, it transforms and
compromises them in their formal identity. It is also there,
subjacent, in the sensuous signs, introducing a sense of
nothingness, even in the joys of sensibility. Time rediscovered,
in its turn, is not alien to time lost; we encounter it at the very
heart of time lost. Lastly, the time regained of art encompasses
and comprehends all the others, for it is only within time
regained that each line of time finds its truth, its place, and its
result form the viewpoint of truth (85-86).

Throughout this chapter we have intentionally left out
Deleuze's discussion of time as it relates to signs. Not only is
there not enough room for it here, but its argument is only
partially developed in *Proust and Signs.* Nonetheless, we are
well aware that every search takes time in order to interpret the
meanings and truths of signs. With regards to the four signs we
have already covered though, we can already trace an outline of
their 'time'. The worldly signs 'waste' our time, because they
establish meaning entirely in a void. Once we have correlated
their origins to them—and they have become objects— we are still
no closer to signifying them. Both their significance and their
temporality are suspended in their objectivity, and thus they do
nothing to further our desires or the course of time. They are
always already a waste of time, for they bring us no joy, as we
have neither understood them, nor their essences.

Similarly, the signs of love evade truth through a
subjective compensation, which means that they also fail to
bring us the proper joys of truth. They too waste our time,
because they supplant this truth with a completely fictitious
understanding of our lover and their world. When eventually the
truth of this world is betrayed by an involuntary sign that we
cannot account for in our subjective understanding, we realize
that our understanding has already 'come too late'. We regret our
understanding, as all the time spent hypothesizing our beloved
could have been spent really getting to know our lover's true
worlds.

Sensuous signs represent a time regained, as they give
us infinite joys while they are searched, conjuring up all sorts of
images and understandings and a plethora of different times. The

time of a quality is therefore a multifarious time, encompassing the respective times of all the series in which it is found. We get a glimpse here of 'eternal' time, of all times simultaneous to each other, and thus come closer to the infinite and eternal truth of the quality's essence (i.e. its actual 'Self').[35]

Finally, in the signs of art we turn entirely towards worldliness, and see the world as composed of infinite truths and times. These overlap in virtuality, where their essences infinitely relate to each other and cause all temporal lines. For as past, present, and future can only be instantiated significantly (and therefore concretely), these essences are eternal and a-temporal, constituting infinite times and durations, without being absolutely expressed by any of them. As the embodiment of essences, art is equally simultaneous to all concrete times and therefore eternal.

The Seventh Criteria:
The Sign's Essence

> [7.] *Essence.* It is only at the profoundest level, on the level of art, that Essence is revealed: as the reason for this relation and for its variations. Then, starting from this final revelation, we can redescend the steps. Not that we would go back into life, into love, into worldliness, but we redescend the series of time by assigning to each temporal line, and to each pieces of signs, the truth appropriate to them. When we have reached the revelation of art, we learn that essence was already there, in the lowest steps and stages. It is essence which, in each case, determined the relation between sign and meaning (87-88).

Arriving at the level of essence, we arrive at pure semiosis, the infinite production of signs and their meanings. These essences are revealed in works of art, whose affects on us display infinite meaning. Searching the signs of art, we come to an intuitive grasp of their materiality and of the virtual essences that have produced these signs and their meanings. It is in this state that all the different times and specific expressions of a sign become simultaneous, as we realize their true causes and powers of materiality.

---

[35] Deleuze capitalizes 'Self' here because it is not a subjective self, but the ideal 'Self', the singularity of one's essence.

From Materiality to
the Concrete

Having traced the progression from materiality to the signs of art, we find that we are now in a position to diagram this movement and give a complete schematic of Deleuze's first concept of the sign. Through this concept, Deleuze has also intentionally sketched an entire ontology, induced from our existential relation to signs and the searches they entail.

The first ontological level is that of materiality. Materiality represents the material unity of the universe, which forms the singular substance of all phenomena. All phenomena are expressed from and within its infinite power. However, the power of materiality is dynamic, differentiated into degrees of power or essences that in turn dynamically relate to each other so as to express various concrete materials. Thus, at very different ontological levels, the unified composition of materiality becomes the multiplicity of essences and their concrete modes (impressions and materials).

In the second ontological realm, the realm of the virtual, the essences express the degrees of materiality's power. In doing so, the essences give materiality reality, as these essences in turn express concrete modes, dividing materiality into materials and instantiating its multiplicity. As the self-organizing powers of materiality, the essences are each virtual machines, the products of which are concrete affects that are an epiphenomena of their virtual effects.

These modes constitute the third ontological tier of the concrete. The concrete is populated by a variety of impressions that are expressions of essential relations. The diversification and difference of every concrete impression corresponds to a virtual effect, a relation of one essence to another or others. Thus, the essences are not metaphysical entities, but inhere within matter, realized in its concrete expression. In addition, they remain infinite and virtual by the fact that no single one of these individual concrete expressions expresses them absolutely. Instead, the multiplicity of concrete materials merely insinuates them, expressing a plurality of virtual machines at work, organizing and individualizing them.

In terms of expression, materiality expresses itself in all virtual essences and all actions/thoughts simultaneously. The virtual essences are expressed, their relations embodied by concrete impressions which in turn implicate each other meaningfully and significantly. However, these meanings and significations are only possible because of and through their relation to the virtual essences underlying them. These virtual essences are what allow us to repeat concrete difference, both in new objects and in abstract meanings and significations. *Hence there are no signs, meanings, or significations that are not both virtually produced at the same time as they are concretely produced*, for a virtual process always inheres within a concrete one.

Secondly, signs gain meaning by implicating each other concretely, yet all these meanings are themselves expressions of the virtual relations that are the truth of these relations. *Therefore, no semiotic expression is ever complete, but only one possible expression of infinite virtual relations at work within it.*

Finally, *thinking is semiosis.* To think is to open the sign up to interpretation or reinterpretation, surveying all the other impressions, signs, and meanings of the world in order to secure meaning. In semiosis, the sign becomes immanent to meaning, which means that it has returned to its essence so that it can unfold from it in a different expression of that essence. Semiosis is the entirely virtual production of signs from out of materiality, through essence. We could also say that it is the perpetual search, that never resolves in a meaning or set of meanings, but in every expression of materiality.

From the Existential
Back to the Material

Through an ontology that differs and differentiates itself virtually, Deleuze has ascribed the ontological priority of *semiosis before semiotics*. Both the semiotic object—which is any meaningful object—and the significant relation of that object, are ontologically preceded by the virtual essences distinguishing and relating them. Prior to any semiotics, these essences relate so as to produce the entire existential field within which semiotics takes place. Further, semiotics is not possible without signs, which motivate the semiotic pursuit and which prompt the search for meaningful relations between materials. This semiosis is the infinite distinction and relation of these materials as signs immanent to objects. Thus, before any semiotic, the essence must be expressed by a concrete infinity of all signs and sign relations, considered only as so many impressions and intuitions, but not as any particular object or action/thought. We can say generally, that *semiosis is the production of objects, while semiotics, succeeding this, produces their significance.*

Part and parcel of semiosis is the search, which is the infinite play of signs within this intuitive field. The search supplants the question of 'what' a sign is (i.e. a semiotic relation) with the more fundamental problem of 'how' a sign emerges in the first place, which is a problem of semiosis, the production of the finite from the infinite. It is also an existential problem, for signs change our relation to materiality, obliging us to modify our worlds. And from this existential perspective, semiotics is as dissatisfying as the sign it attempts to place, as it fails to reveal the essences causing all of them. The traditional discipline of semiotics is flawed insofar as it conceptualizes the sign after this entire production, as if the sign always already had a significant meaning (e.g. Saussure's declaration that a sign "designates" a "*signification* and *signal*". Despite the fact that the relation between the two is "arbitrary", Saussure holds that both are nonetheless *necessary* for the constitution of a sign (Sausure: 67). In this way, the sign becomes merely an expression and function of significance, instead of that which constitutes significations in the first place, the very 'signing' or 'semiosis' of the sign itself. But signs are never completely captured by significance, and are always available to new significant and insignificant relations:

> We are wrong to believe in facts; there are only signs. We are
> wrong to believe in truth; there are only interpretations. The
> sign is an ever-equivocal, implicit, and implicated meaning
> (Deleuze 1972: 90).

As we have seen, the sign complicates meaning and signification, without adhering to any one of them. One has only to search the sign again to discover new meanings for it that it always already implies. Our thinking about the sign never ends so long as we continue to let it keep 'signing', unfolding and creating new signs and meanings along the way:

> What forces us to think is the sign. The sign is the object of an encounter; but it is precisely the contingency of the encounter which guarantees the necessity of what it leads us to think. The act of thinking does not proceed from a simple natural possibility; on the contrary, it is the only true creation. Creation is the genesis of the act of thinking within thought itself. This genesis implicates something which does violence to thought, which wrests it from its natural stupor, and its merely abstract possibilities. To think is always to interpret-to explicate, to develop, to decipher, to translate a sign. Translating, deciphering, developing are each creations... We seek the truth only within time, constrained and forced. The truth-seeker is the jealous man who catches a lying sign on the beloved's face. He is the sensitive man, in that he encounters the violence of an impression. He is the reader, the auditor, in that the work of art emits signs which will perhaps force him to create, like the call of genius to other geniuses. The work of art is born from signs as much as it generates them; the creator is like the jealous man, interpreter of the god, who scrutinizes the sign in which the truth *betrays itself*...In science and in philosophy, the intelligence always "comes before"; but characteristic of signs is their appeal to this intelligence insofar as it comes after, insofar as it must come after. The same is true of memory: the sensuous signs force us to seek their truth, but hereby mobilize an involuntary memory (or an involuntary imagination born of desire). Finally the signs of art force us to think: they mobilize pure thought as a faculty of essences. They release within thought what depends least on its good will: the act of thinking itself (162-164).

As we can see in this passage, thought follows from the truth, but the harbinger of both truth and thought is the sign. The sign is our immediate existential relation to the truth, which we search in order to establish various thoughts. If this relation is 'contingent', it is because we never know in advance what will strike us as a sign. We are assaulted by an invisible essence, which grasps us precisely at the limit of our intelligence and changes the thought that we think. There is a difference in kind here: 'thinking' (i.e. the verb, the act of 'thought') is the virtual contact of worlds with essences. It is heralded by the sign, which is searched (i.e. thought about) in order to establish a significant relation of the sign to our worlds (viz. in meaning, significance, and intelligence). While the individual 'thoughts' that we think are what are produced by this act (i.e. the noun: the various objects, meanings, significations, intelligences, worlds, ideas, voluntary memories, etc.). And just as thoughts follow from thinking, thinking itself follows from the sign, while the sign in turn follows from the violence of the essence, which comes from outside of everything we know (Deleuze *Logic*: 183-184).

Now if thought always comes from outside us, and if it is only ever 'betrayed' or accidentally revealed by involuntary signs, memories, or imaginations, how are we to encourage thinking and its creative capacity? In *Proust and Signs*, Deleuze has left us several clues as to what we can do to encourage thought; however these remain in a rather convoluted and general form. Nonetheless, we can still identify some of the major traits of thinking.

To begin with, the process of thinking insignificantly creates new signs and impressions that are completely unfamiliar, and violent for that reason. These strange new impressions must be apprenticed to in their own right, through a sustained repetition of the thought process, which not only produces these signs, but which correlates them meaningfully to each other and to other objects. As thinking is inseparable from this violence, Deleuze tells us, "One must be endowed for the signs, ready to encounter them, one must open oneself to their violence" (166). This implies that as one apprentices to the truth, one must be violent with one's own understandings and embrace signs at every opportunity. Every sign must be taken up and pursued for as long as it takes to produce another sign. In this way, the series of understanding are continually broken and a perpetual reformulation of knowledge is enacted according to these new signs and their subsequent significations. In effect, one multiplies their knowledge, but also thwarts their own series of understandings from becoming a consistent whole by maintaining a constant breach of knowledge by the truth. Consequently, we succumb to a perpetual dissatisfaction with every sign's meaning, but conjunctively experience the perpetual joys of discovering all these meanings and of finding new signs from which we can draw even more.

We know from experience that by contemplating any concrete action/thought for long enough, it begins to take on a different light. We have all caught ourselves coming back to the same object only to find it 'looking differently' or to find that we see something different in it than we have ever seen before. The more we think about an action/thought, the more likely it is to present itself as a sign and prompt a search. Thus, by aggressively questioning our own understandings, we may in fact stumble upon a sign and return to the process of thought.

Both the search and the sign come from out of the virtual essence that differentiates them. Neither has ontological priority, both emerging simultaneously through their common essence. However, we can reach this essence faster by exhausting our intelligence, continually abstracting it from itself so that its implications are stretched to proportions that simply cannot sustain themselves and which even begin to contradict themselves. As logic and abstraction follow the significant chains of the intelligent series, extracting and abstracting certain portions of them into compound series and individual worlds, this process merely multiplies our intelligence from within itself. It therefore codifies intelligence, making it more stringent and absolute, and excluding all other series from these worlds and abstractions. In contrast, to genuinely think, one must find new signs which have no place in these codes, thus forcing their rupture. Ironically, one way of forcing this rupture is to make these codes as rigid as possible, so that everything threatens them. To insist on absolute meanings without compromises will, at its limit, result in a world for every object, which would be nothing more than a schizophrenic conundrum of infinite objects (i.e. materiality itself!). Through the objective formula (which dictates that every impression must necessarily correspond to one object, and one object only), the object (which is always already composed of multiple impressions) becomes divided against itself, such that its impressions immediately reach their own limit and become the signs of something else.

By constantly pursuing the limits of our intelligence, and attempting to reach that which is more abstract than these abstractions, we may end up inducing thought.[36] And so, where everything is meaningful, we must ask what the meaning of everything is, pushing intelligence to a higher degree, abstracting it deliriously so that we force it outside itself, into its external materiality. Entire worlds become qualities in this process, signing the infinite mutation of these worlds into different ones, outside and between the ones we know.

This process cannot be 'willed' insofar as one cannot consciously preconceive what the search of a sign will reveal. The most we can do is concentrate on our dissatisfaction with a particular object or meaning, in order to resubmit it to a search to discover more about it. Thus, although thinking is involuntary, this is not to say that thinking is determined, but quite the opposite. Only voluntary intelligence is determined, inscribed in codes and over-codes that sustain its meaning. Intelligence represents a determinism of meaning, though one which contains within itself endless contradictions that prevent it from ever closing itself completely. Thinking, on the other hand, is prior to code and meaning and therefore undetermined insofar as it solicits the infinity of materiality, which preexists concrete determination, and which simultaneously is expressed by the infinity of all meanings (and therefore all determinations).

Now, although Deleuze's concept of the sign begins with an existential analysis, there is little in his theory that could be called *existentialist* (at least in its resemblance to Sartre, Heidegger, Camus, etc.). Signs emerge before us as much by 'choice' as 'spontaneously' from out of materiality. Yet, every time we 'choose' to 'project ourselves' into this apprenticeship, we make a 'leap' into the unknown. The search of every sign is an encounter with the void, wherein we have no definite notion of what will be the outcome of it. As much as we are 'thrown' into the world, we are thrown into the search of it, and this is facilitated by signs that act like road markers in a foreign land. Notions of choice and projection can only be formulated after

---

[36] Deleuze and Guattari allude to this in *Thousand Plateaus*: "Our criticism of these linguistic models is not that they are too abstract but, on the contrary, that they are not abstract enough..." (7).

this leap, insofar as they are significantly judged and therefore follow from these insignificant encounters.

Unfamiliar and daunting, every sign repeats this 'thrownness', and its feeling is always the vertigo of being at the threshold of a new world which may or may not destroy us. Signs remind us of the suppleness of our knowledge, our worlds, and our egos. Delicately, they hang in balance with one another, just barely warding off the angst and chaos of death. But this is never some complete and final death, some mortality or biological end. This is the infinite death of our individuality, which happens every time we explore a sign and we learn something new. As all signs mark the boundary and limit of chaos, every sign represents death in some degree. What perishes with every sign is at least one series of subjective understanding and therefore at least one small ego, one small trace of individuality. As we suffer signs, we succumb to all the little deaths, these becomings of new personalities and worlds, which erase and copy themselves over-top of the old ones. Yet, we also experience all the joys and pleasures of building ourselves anew and discovering new meaning and new possibilities in the world. For every little death, anxiety, and pain, there is the ecstasy of the sign and its essence, which needs only be searched in order to restore ourselves beyond ourselves, and our previous joys to greater ones.

Chapter V

To Imagine Spinoza: Deleuze and the Materiality of the Sign

The Philosophic Collage

For Deleuze, every work of literature is an "assemblage", a "multiplicity" of different "dates", "speeds", "functions", and abstract ideas that intersect in the work so as to produce different effects (Deleuze 1987: 3-4). Insofar as literature can affect our minds and institutions, writing *functions*, every literary work acting like a "little machine" composed of parts pilfered from other ones (4). The "literary machine" brings into communication a "war machine, love machine, revolutionary machine", "bureaucratic machine", and others, interrupting their previous functions so as to posit them in new directions (4-5). In effect, it cuts away parts of these other assemblages and multiplicities in order 'to stick' (in French, *coller*) them together in a new arrangement, a '*collage*' of their former mechanics.

From this perspective, every piece of philosophic literature must be evaluated according to its component singularities and the machines that they are borrowed or stolen from. Deleuze is the first to admit that he is a philosophic "collage artist" and that his philosophic works are admixtures of concepts drawn from fine art, music, literature, the history of philosophy, and innumerable other sources (Deleuze 2004: 144). He even boasts that he has striven for what he calls philosophic "buggery", hoping to give each philosopher he analyzes, "a child that would be his own offspring, yet monstrous" (Deleuze 1990 *Negotiations*: 6). In this way, Deleuze fuses great thinkers together into philosophic mutations that are uniquely his own: Nietzsche-Spinoza, Bergson-Proust, Freud-Marx, etc. (Deleuze & Parnet 1987: 15-18). These are no mere comparisons; rather they are collages of arguments, ideas, and concepts that Deleuze has scavenged from these pedagogues and others. By the time Spinoza gets dragged into this philosophical chop-shop, Deleuze has already cut-up Hume, Peirce, Proust, and Bergson, from whom he has developed an elaborate semiotic theory. His book, *Proust and Signs* represents the culmination of these studies, while the two works that follow it, *Expressionism in Philosophy: Spinoza* and *Difference and Repetition* (released in the same year), represent the next phase of his semiotics.

A self professed "Spinozist", Deleuze borrows the greater part of Spinoza's ontology and epistemology and grafts them on to his own material realism (Deleuze and Guattari 1987: 253).[37] Deleuze is able to make this philosophic conjunction by equating the material substratum of his universe with Spinoza's 'substance' or 'God'.[38] Accordingly, he is forced to situate the sign within that ontological scheme, which inadvertently obliges him to shift from an existential analysis of its phenomenon (like that of Proust's)[39] towards a concept that is also consistent with Spinoza's arguments.[40] In this way, Deleuze continues to ratify his existential and empirical accounts of signs, while at the same time pursuing an ontology that compliments them.

---

[37] By 'material realist' we mean a materialism that is both monistic and 'neutral', a 'neutral monism' being a monism that is not just physical (i.e. expressed in 'extension' or 'body') or ideal (i.e. expressed 'in mind'), but which expresses both thought and extension, in addition to infinite other attributes (Stubenberg 2005). Žižeck is also quick to point out that "this absolutely neutral medium of the multitude of attributes... [is] thoroughly *neutral* with regard to their "good" or "bad" effects", as these effects precede such "subjective" judgments (Žižeck 2004: 34).

[38] An unabashedly atheistic interpretation of Spinoza, reflecting perhaps Deleuze's own religious sentiments, and his deep affiliation with Marxism.

[39] From 1953 until the 1968 publication of *Spinoza: Expressionism in Philosophy*, Deleuze investigated the sign and its relation to signification in nearly all his works. Further, the majority of Deleuze's articles, books, and reviews were on 'existential' philosophers: Heidegger, Sartre, Nietzsche, Marcel, Hyppolite, Merleau-Ponty, Bergson, Sacher-Masoch, Proust, and others.

[40] This is not to say that Deleuze abandons his existential work. Contrariwise, in *Difference and Repetition* he indulges in a complete phenomenological reduction of signs and communication. See his account of the "signal-sign system" (Deleuze 1994: 222).

It is the intention of this paper, therefore, to trace these semiotic arguments, and to show how his existential interpretation of the sign relates to a complete ontology of its phenomenon. In a Deleuzian spirit, this paper is itself a collage of his many works, the juxtaposition of which exposes a thoroughly developed theory of the sign that is at the heart of his ontology, epistemology, and ethics. Extending its implications, we discover that Deleuze's semiotics is actually an ethical prescription, wherein he proposes the search of signs as a means of living in accordance with universal truth.

Deleuze's Existential Argument for the Sign

Previously, in *Proust and Signs*, Deleuze observed that a sign appears before us as "sensuous impression", with some "feeling" super-added to it, such as "nervous exaltation", or other "joys" and "sufferings" (Deleuze 1972: 7, 11-12). The sign unnerves us because we are unaware of its implications, yet at the same time it can bring us prodigious joy when we finally discover its significance. Concealing some invisible relation to the world, it fills us with nervousness and anxiety, these apprehensions arising in the face of its unknown potential. In order to escape these unpleasant feelings, we search for the sign's meaning so that we can surpass its mere appearance and being-there and come to some knowledge of it. Thus, the first thesis of *Proust and Signs* is that signs make us anxious and that this anxiety plays itself out in a search that is "to be taken in the strong sense of the term, as we say "the search for truth" " (3-4). Despite whatever memories or preconceived understandings we have of that which appears before us as a sign, we do not know its full significance. As we search a sign, we begin to apprentice to this truth, relating the sign to the other actions and thoughts we know. However, regardless of whatever objects or significations we associate with the sign through that search, it always already exceeds this meaning. First, because the sign engenders the very search for its meaning and thus announces itself before whatever objects or significations we meaningfully relate to it. Secondly, even after these meanings have been established, there is nothing to stop a sign from continuing to sign. Its existential compulsion can arise at any time and in any context, promoting a new search for a different understanding. Thus, the sign not only precedes its own meaning, but succeeds it as well, making it constantly available to new meaning and therefore always already signifying something else.

Instead, it is as if the sign's truth is lodged in a concealed 'essence' that is external to its phenomenon. This essence is not only revealed by the sign and its various meanings, but by our compulsion to search the sign for more, as if the sign's significance were constantly evolving. If the first thesis of *Proust and Signs* is that the sign is a search for truth, its second thesis is that both the sign's impression and its multifarious significances veil an invisible essence inhering within them, which constitutes this truth:

> At the end of the Search, the interpreter understands what had escaped him... that the material meaning is nothing without an ideal essence which it incarnates.... [T]hese signs, as though *dematerialized*, find their meaning in an ideal essence (13).

As we have seen, the sensitive and emotional impressions of a sign lead us to search for the sign's meaning. Doing so, we relate it to other impressions, so that it becomes a particular 'matter' for the mind, a 'formed' (i.e. meaningful) object or idea. However, if we try to signify that which distinguishes our impressions from each other and 'forms' them into meaningful relations with one another, we are at a loss. Consequently, Deleuze says that the expressive power that distinguishes and forms our impressions into objects and ideas is *de*material in that it both forms and *de*forms particular materials (i.e. thoughts and actions) without being represented by them. This essence, however, is not metaphysical; rather it is "immaterial" in the sense that it is *im*manent to actions and thoughts, without ever being definitively expressed by any one of them (40-41).

In light of Deleuze's adamant materialism, his use of the words 'dematerialized' and 'immaterial' may seem puzzling. However, if we interpret them in the sense of 'not having form', or a material force as of yet without relevant meaning or shape, it makes sense. The prefix '*im*-' in '*im*material' should therefore be taken in the Latin sense of 'towards' and not as 'lack' or 'not'. Similarly the prefix '*de*-' in '*de*materialized' should be take in the Latin/old French sense of 'apart' or 'away' (viz. from concrete and formed materials). What is immaterial and dematerialized would not be metaphysical, nor would it transcend materiality, rather it would only transcend whatever form we try to ascribe to it, as it is perpetually in the state of becoming formed. Thus, every essence is entirely physical and material, but formless and invisible, positing forms without ever being definitively expressed by them. Inasmuch as every essence precedes and posits the impressions and meanings of signs, essences therefore constitute the 'truth" of signs, the eternally productive powers that give rise to all their distinct modes.[41]

As herald of the truth then, the sign occupies a rather unique place in the Deleuze's early ontological work, existing at the threshold between the emergence of the concrete expressions of essences, but also at the point at which we can pass beyond them, into the pure expression of their differences. The sign always faces two realms: one concrete, material, and productive, the other immaterial and essential to its production. Or shall we say, the sign always has two sides: the impression producing and the essence produced by it:

> All production starts from the impression, because only the impression unites in itself the accident of the encounter and the necessity of the effect, a violence which it obliges us to undergo. Thus all production starts from a sign, and supposes the depth and darkness of the involuntary... The Search is indeed the production of the sought-for truth (130-131).

---

[41] In order to distinguish Deleuze's concept of essence from classical 'essentialism', DeLanda opts to call them "*dynamical processes*", which are "*immanent* to the world of matter and energy" (DeLanda 2002: 3). Essences are neither 'forms' nor sets of particular properties, as "Deleuze replaces the false genesis implied by these pre-existing forms which remain *the same* for all time, with a theory of morphogenesis based on the notion of *the different*. He conceives difference not negatively, as a lack of resemblance, but positively or productively, as that which drives a dynamical process" (4). In this way, the infinite difference and dynamism of essences produces equally infinite modes of thought and action that are as unique as their essences.

The sign assaults us with anxiety, compelling us to search for its meaning. This violence is produced through our search for the sign's essence, the 'sought-for truth' eluding us, which leads us into the involuntary, invisible, and ideal realm of its cause (Deleuze 1991: 41).

Expressionism and the
Virtual Monism of Substance

Like Spinoza before him, Deleuze conceives of the universe as a 'neutral monism',[42] a single substance that expresses *everything*. Limited by the existential argument he embarks on in *Proust and Signs*, Deleuze can only describe this substance in those terms, likening it to "the surface of the Earth", "the world of difference", "the instantaneous image of eternity", or the "multiplicity of chaos" that precedes all phenomena (Deleuze 1972: 41, 62, 149).[43] By merging his existential investigations with Spinoza's arguments though, Deleuze is able to ground his ideas in a complete ontology. He then uses this ontology to explain how signs and other materials are manifested from out of substance and why it is that signs have such peculiar effects on us.

In order to bridge his own thoughts with Spinoza's, Deleuze begins by arguing that although substance is expressed as different actions and thoughts, the plurality of these materials attests to "*internalized difference, which becomes immanent*" (viz. immanent to those materials) (59). Were actions and thoughts not differentiated, the universe would remain an amorphous totality. As this is not the case, the "essence" of substance must entail the "absolutely" infinite "power" of differentiating all modes from each other (Spinoza 1992: 31, 56).[44] Thus, the essence of substance is an internal power of

---

[42] See footnote 37.

[43] Deleuze has several other phrases for this phenomenon, including "involuntary memory", "*the very being of the past in itself*", "truth", "internalized difference", "essence", "original time", "an absolute primordial time, a veritable eternity which unites sign and meaning", and "a kind of superior *viewpoint*, an irreducible viewpoint which signifies at once the birth of the world and the original character of a world" (Deleuze 1972: 56-60, 86, 98).

[44] "God's power is his very essence."

"[d]ifference and repetition" (Deleuze 1972: 65), which is in turn divided into finite degrees (i.e. 'essences') that are repeated and "constituted" in the concrete (i.e. as particular actions and thoughts) (Spinoza 1992: 37).[45]

The apparent duality between essences and modes is actually the result of the tripartite relation that takes place between substance, its essences, and its attributes. Deleuze argues that the key to uncovering this relationship lies in Spinoza's emphasis on the role of 'expression' that occurs between these three. Substance, essences, and attributes together constitute a "triad" of expression, all three separated by differences in kind:

> Infinite essences are distinguished through the attributes in which they find expression, but are identified in the substance to which they relate. We everywhere confront the necessity of distinguishing three terms: substance which expresses itself, the attribute which expresses, and the essence which is expressed. It is through attributes that essence is distinguished from substance, but through essence that substance is itself distinguished from attributes: a triad each of whose terms serves as a middle term relating the two others, in three syllogisms (Deleuze 2005: 27-28).

An absolutely infinite substance expresses an infinite array of particular essences that are expressed in infinite attributes (Spinoza 1992: 37 and 43).[46]

Now, as any particular essence is expressed in all attributes, it is important to understand that these attributes "express themselves in one and the same order, down to the level of finite modes, which must have the same order in different attributes. This identity of order defines a correspondence of modes: to any mode of one attribute there necessarily corresponds a mode of each of the other attributes" (Deleuze 2005: 106). This is "Spinoza's first formulation of parallelism: there is an *identity of order* or *correspondence*

---

[45] *Ethics*, I, Def. 6, explication; and I, 11.

[46] *Ethics*, I, 11 and 16.

between modes of different attributes" (107).[47] For example, an essence expressed in the attribute of extension becomes an action, while concurrently the same essence expressed in the attribute of thought becomes an impression of the mind. Deleuze notes that the term "parallelism" actually belongs to Leibniz (Spinoza never used the term), but that it "adequately characterizes Spinoza's philosophy" too, though Spinoza's parallelism is much more "strict" than Leibniz's (Deleuze 2005: 107-109). Leibniz's parallelism implies only a "correspondence" between "substances and phenomena, solids and projections" (108). In opposition, Spinoza's parallelism is much more profound:

> Modes of different attributes are one and the same modification, differing only in attribute. Through this identity of being or ontological unity, Spinoza refuses the intervention of a transcendent God to make each term in one series agree with a term in the other, or even to set the series in agreement through their unequal principles. Spinoza's doctrine is rightly named "parallelism," but this is because it refuses any analogy, any eminence, any kind of superiority of one series. Parallelism, strictly speaking, is to be understood neither from the viewpoint of occasional causes, nor from the viewpoint of ideal causality, but only from the viewpoint of an immanent God and immanent causality (109).

The essences of substance do not transcend the attributes, but remain immanent to them, as every essential relation immediately modifies every attribute. The profundity of Spinoza's parallelism lies in the fact that it is "ontological": every essential relation is paralleled in every attribute, so that between both levels monism is retained (Deleuze 1988: 86).

In order to expound upon the relation between essence and attribute, Deleuze uses Proust's famous formula: essences are " "real without being present, ideal without being abstract." " (Deleuze 1972: 60). An essence is intangible until differentiated

---

[47] Deleuze references the *Ethics*, II, 17 & Scholium for further proof of this argument (Spinoza 1992: 77-78).

in the attributes, at which point its power becomes a particular modification of those attributes (27-28).

This being the case, Deleuze calls these essences "virtual", as their invisible relations are concealed within the concrete modes that express them in the attributes. The term is borrowed Bergson, who argued that all our "memory-images" are derived from a "pure" past, which informs our memory images 'virtually', but which is lost forever in time (Bergson 1991: 131-134). Our past is always there alongside us, though it is never revealed directly, but only through our present actions and thoughts. Likewise, the essences are neither transcendent nor transitive and can be called virtual in that they are instantiated by a plethora of concrete materials without being completely revealed by any one of these materials. There is no metaphysical divide between virtual essences and their concrete modes, rather the virtual is inherent-within and immanent-to the concrete modes that they express (Deleuze 1991: 41).

Understanding the relation between the virtual and the concrete is key to dissolving some of the attacks that have been launched against Deleuze, in particular Badiou's criticism that Deleuze's interpretation of Spinoza sets up a "metaphysics of the One" (Badiou 2000: 10, 16) that is "classical in nature (a metaphysics of Being and of the ground)" (54). This critique arises because of a rather superficial reading of Deleuze. First, expressionism nullifies traditional metaphysics by making the transcendental immanent to thought and action. In *The Logic of Sense*, Deleuze is very clear about where this "transcendental field" fits into his ontology:

> Metaphysical surface (*transcendental field*) is the name that will be given to the frontier established, on one hand, between bodies taken together as a whole and inside the limits which envelop them, and on the other, propositions in general (125).

In other words, the transcendental field is synonymous with the 'virtual' in that it is the surface of concrete production (208), the "pure Event" of this concrete production (238) and the 'becoming' of the concrete (i.e. the "verb" (241)) which is 'unconscious' and "pre-individual" (244), but which results in the "signification" of individual thoughts (241). In effect, the metaphysical is a virtual relation of those essences of thought that all our significant ideas express. Contra Badiou then, the virtual is not "beyond" (45) the concrete, but only beyond signification. Thus, Deleuze's metaphysics should not be interpreted as that which ontologically transcends concrete ideas, sensations, and emotions, but as the immeasurable physical and mental acts that we perform so as to posit them. As we will argue later, although these acts may be phenomenologically amorphous (i.e. formless), we nonetheless experience them in concrete intuitions that are true experiences of the essences causing them. Thus, the 'beyond' of the physical that is the 'metaphysical' does not come from outside the physical (i.e. outside materiality) or from some negation of the physical, but is the act of 'going beyond' our finite ideas of the world through the eternal production of new experiences.[48] Metaphysics is therefore the intuition of virtual, the transcendence of finitely physical things (i.e. formed impression; significant thoughts and actions) through infinitely physical acts (i.e. thinking and acting).[49]

The Two Senses of Signs and the Parallelism of Attributes

Employing expressionism to signs, Deleuze argues that (in ontological order) the monism of 'the world' or 'substance' expresses essences, which are expressed in various concrete materials, of which signs are but one type. Calling them "sensuous impressions", Deleuze implies that these are signs of both the body and the mind, for other bodies impress upon ours and modify it, but these modifications are known only to us through sensations that are realized in the mind (i.e. our essence

---

[48] We should therefore read the prefix '*meta-*' in '*meta*physics' according to the Greek sense of that which exists 'beside' the physical , rather than that which comes 'after' it.

[49] When Marcel remarks, "Is not that which you call "recollection" the same as what others have termed "intuition"?", he recognizes that our experience of Bergson's 'virtual' past is intuitive, and that every present recollection is part of the infinite act of the becoming of the past in and through what we are conscious of presently. In recollection, our present ideas are transcended by means of an intuition of our immanent pure past (Marcel: 25).

in the attribute of thought) (Deleuze 1972: 7). Accordingly, we should take the expression 'sensuous impression' in two senses: a physical impression on the body that occurs in parallel to sensations and ideas in the mind (the former in the attribute of extension, the latter in the attribute of thought). For example, if one is hit with a snowball, their body not only changes position, but reacts with electrochemical 'signs' that pass throughout the nervous system, triggering all sorts of physical reactions (flushed skin, swelling, elevated heart-rate, etc.). The series of these bodily reactions and counter-reactions constitute the body's 'search' of the foreign object. Meanwhile, the mind correlatively experiences painful feelings and visual impressions (e.g. slush on the skin), all of which are signs that lead us in a mental search for a meaningful notion of what has happened to our body (e.g. 'I have been hit!').

Thus, there are at least two senses of signs.[50] On the one hand, the sign could be a physical/bodily 'affection' in the attribute of extension, while on the other it is a mental 'affect' in the attribute of thought, both of which come from the same essential relation, or 'effect':

> A sign, according to Spinoza, can have several meanings, but it is always an *effect*. An effect is first of all the trace of one body upon another, the state of a body insofar as it suffers the action of another body. It is an *affectio* [i.e. an affection] - for example, the effect of the sun on our body, which "indicates" the nature of the affected body and merely "envelops" the nature of the affecting body. We have knowledge of our affections through the ideas we have, sensations or perceptions, sensations of heat and color, the perception of form and distance ... We will call them *affects* [i.e. *affectus*] strictly speaking (Deleuze 1997: 138-139).
>
> It has been remarked that as a general rule the affection (*affectio*) is said directly of the body, while the affect (*affectus*) refers to the mind (Deleuze 1988: 49).[51]

---

[50] Deleuze actually comes up with "six signs, or seven" (Deleuze 1997: 138-140).
[51] Deleuze here clarifies Spinoza's rather ambiguous use of these terms. For more on this ambiguity, see Samuel Shirley's introduction to Spinoza (Spinoza 1992: 23-24).

The affection is not just the effect of one extended body on another, but is necessarily a collision of their essences too, for in actuality essences must be extended in order to be related to each other. Every essence is inseparable from a body, which is related to others in the attribute of extension (Spinoza 1992: 72-73).[52] Deleuze, therefore, reserves the term 'effect' for the relation of essences, and 'affections' for the physical modifications their extended bodies undergo. Every effect (i.e. every essential relation) becomes various 'affections' in the bodies involved (e.g. physical and physiological changes).

In like manner, effects and their affections happen in parallel with modifications in the attribute of thought. In order not to confuse their senses (extended and thought), Deleuze reserves the term 'effect' for an essential relation in extension, while in turn he calls an 'Idea' the exact same essential relation as it applies to modifications of thought (Deleuze 1994: 24-27).[53] As a convention, Deleuze generally capitalizes 'Idea' when he refers to its essential sense, and leaves it in lower case when referring to a concrete 'idea' of the mind. The Idea of our essence related to another has the virtual effect of affecting (*afficere*; the verb: to affect) our mind with various 'affects' (e.g. sensations, feelings, signs, significant ideas, etc.). Thus, 'effects' are to affections in the attribute of extension, what 'Ideas' are affects, images, and significant ideas in the attribute of thought, the two terms merely differing in ontological sense (Spinoza 1992: 80; Deleuze 1988: 48-51).

Essence, Truth, and Signs

Insofar as our essence is infinitely related to other essences, our body undergoes effects and suffers affections, while our mind undergoes Ideas and suffers affects. Thus, the

---

[52] Literally these collide in Spinoza, for bodies are distinguished by their speeds in the attribute of extension, just as their essences are distinguished as Ideas in the attribute of thought, and fundamentally as degrees of power in reference to substance Itself. See *Ethics*, II, 13, Lemma 1 (Spinoza 1992: 72-73).

[53] Here Deleuze draws the distinction between *i*deas and *I*deas, though sadly he is not consistent with this denotation in many of his other writings, including those on Spinoza. Accordingly, in what follows we will edit his writings to illustrate the discrepancy.

truth of any given affection or affect lies in its effect or Idea respectively, for they belong to one and the same essential relation that simultaneously unites the modes of these parallel attributes. In that all essences are extended and related in the bodies they engender, bodies have effects on each other that are necessarily true and which cause true affections in them.[54] Yet, in our efforts to think the true Idea of our affects and affections, we run into difficulty:

> In one sense, a sign is always the idea of an effect apprehended under conditions that separate it from its causes. Thus the effect of a body on ours is not apprehended relative to the essence of our body and the essence of the external body, but in terms of a momentary state of our variable constitution and a simple presence of the thing whose nature we do not know (*Ethics,* II, 17). Such signs are *indicative*: they are *effects of mixture.* They indicate the state of our body primarily, and the presence of the external body secondarily (Deleuze 1988: 105-107).

As the mind struggles to unravel the meaning of its affects and the true Ideas behind them, it searches them as signs. Yet, each sign/affect is a subjective impression that is relative to *our* essence, in both body and mind, which means that it can only reveal the essence of the other's body or mind "secondarily", which is to say, analogously or abductively from *our* perspective. For example, imagine we are touched by another person. In the attribute of extension, the essence of our body meets that of the other. The extended effect is that our bodies physically change, setting in motion different physiological reactions in us both. Meanwhile, in the attribute of thought, we both feel and think about this touch differently. Conceiving the touch in our own ways, our respective affects are nonetheless all signs of the same ideal touch, the same Idea of our essential encounter. As we try to understand this Idea though, we fall short, for we do not share the same essential mind and can only

---

[54] Hence Spinoza's insistence on the supremacy of the body over the mind in both the *Ethics* and the *Treatise.* See *Ethics*, II, 19-30 (Spinoza 1992: 80-85); and *Treatise*, 21, 33, and 74 (Spinoza 1992: 237-8, 240, 252).

imagine what the other is feeling from what we feel (i.e. 'secondarily').

Now, when Spinoza tells us that a "true idea must agree with that of which it is the idea (*ideatum*)" (Spinoza 1992: 32), or that a "true idea must agree with its Ideate" (Spinoza 1992: 52),[55] he means that in order for our ideas to be true, they would somehow have to correspond to the essences of thought they express — Ideas. The Ideas that are the truth of our affects concern our essence as it relates to all others in the attribute of thought. In contrast, the ideas we contemplate (*ideata*) are the concrete manifestations of these Ideas (*Ideates*), the meaningful and finite significations of their modes.

An Idea is never a simple impression, never a "dumb thing like a picture on a tablet" (Spinoza 1992: 91-92). Rather, an Idea is the "the very act of understanding" (Spinoza 1992: 91-92), the active relation of our essence to others, which unfolds as a series of affects. These affects are then associated into finite ideas: meaningful objects, significant expressions, or any other "conception[s] of thought" (Spinoza 1992: 95-96):

> The idea is representative. But we have to distinguish the [I]dea that we are (the mind as idea of the body) from the ideas that we have. The [I]dea that we are is in God; God possesses [I]t adequately, not just insofar as he constitutes us, but in that he is affected with an infinity of different [I]deas ([I]deas of the other essences that all agree with ours, and of the other [essential] existences that are causes of ours without limit). Therefore we do not have this [I]dea immediately. The only ideas we have under the nature conditions of our perception are the ideas that represent what happens to our body, the effect of another body on ours, that is, a mixing of both bodies. They are necessarily inadequate (II, 11, 12, 19, 24, 25, 26, 27 ...).
>
> Such ideas are images. Or rather, images are the corporeal affections themselves (*affectio*), the traces of an external body on our body. Our ideas are therefore ideas of images or affections that represent a state of things, that is, by which we affirm the presence of the external body so long as

---

[55] Shirley's translation notes are very enlightening on this point (Spinoza 1992: 25). See also Deleuze 1988: 73-76.

our body remains affected in this way (II,17): 1. Such ideas are *signs;* they are not *explained* by our essence or power, but *indicate* our actual state and our incapacity to rid ourselves of a trace; they do not *express* the essence of the external body, but *indicate* the presence of this body and its effect on us (II, 16) (Deleuze 1988: 73-74).

The "[I]dea that we are (the mind as idea of the body)" is our essence as it exists Ideally in God's thought, virtually related to all other essences and constituting a particular degree of His power. God's Idea of us is 'adequate' because it is the knowledge of our extended essence as it relates to all others, a direct knowledge of their effects on us. Contrariwise, the immediate ideas that we think are "inadequate" because they confuse the affects of these effects with others and thus represent these extended effects in an indirect 'image' that is merely a play of affects on affects. Affects being mere 'traces' of effects, the images and ideas formed from them tell us nothing about the true bodies and essences affecting us.

Truth being dynamic and infinite, we must look outside the finite images and ideas of intellect for it. This is where signs come in. Signs are a very special breed of modes, not only because they force us out of our understandings, but also because they are the only impressions that can be infinitely interpreted and searched. In this way, signs are the only modes that manifest the infinity of essential relation, which means that they must share an immediate proximity to the essences causing them. Signs therefore act as a bridge between the immaterial realm of essences and the material world that we experience, marking the threshold of emerging actions and thoughts, the border where essential Ideas become the existential affects and ideas that we perceive.

For the most part though, signs have only a remote relation to their Ideas. This is due to the fact that signs assume meaning only when they are related to other affects of thought. Essences express affects (including signs), but these concrete differences can only be concretely differentiated in relation to each other. Almost paradoxically, the sign-as-affect only becomes a meaningful expression when it is therefore expressed in terms of the affects of essences other than its own. By linking with other affects in this way, the sign gains specific associations that give it a place in the world. Yet this specific place and meaning comes at the sacrifice of the sign's greater truth, namely its own essence, which infinitely relates it to an infinity of others.

In signification and its various forms (images, codes, propositions, abstractions, etc.), nothing new is expressed, rather affects are repeated to each other as expressions of expressions, modes of modes. The sign signifies its material, just as that material signifies it, in a completely superfluous expression whose truth is external (Deleuze & Guattari 1987: 112). Whatever significant thought or action we give them is more like an expression of these essences 'twice removed': removed once in the sign, which is only a chimera of a true and essential Idea; removed again in our finite idea of that sign, which represents this trace with the affect of a completely different essence. We signify signs in the hopes understanding their essences, but rather ironically we find that instead these ideas do nothing but lead us away from their essences towards the affects of others. Thus, we can say that *signifiance* (i.e. the act of *signing*; the becoming of the sign) and *signification* (i.e. the act of *signifying*; the finite being of the sign) are different in kind from each other and become a conflict that is symbolized by the sign. The sign signifies infinitely, but it is never adequately signified by anything.

From Signs to Essences: Qualities

Insofar as infinite essential relations become affects, one discovers the essential when "one looks, *a priori*, for qualities conceived as unlimited, or, setting out from what is limited, one looks, *a posteriori*, for qualities that may be taken to infinity, which are as it were "involved" in the limits of the finite" (Deleuze 2005: 45-46). Whereby infinite qualities can only be the expressions of similarly infinite essential relations, these unlimited qualities indicate them *a priori*. However, the unlimited significance of these qualities is only realized when they are searched *a posteriori* as infinite signs. Unlimited qualities/signs allude to essential infinity, but only so long as we continue to search them and sustain their infinite signifiance. In *Proust and Signs*, Deleuze calls infinite qualities "sensuous" signs, both because they are affects of the senses, and because the 'sense' of these qualities belongs to a multiplicity of objects:

> It may happen that the sensuous quality gives us a strange joy at the same time that it transmits a kind of imperative. Thus experienced, the quality no longer appears as a property of the object which now possesses it, but as the sign of an *altogether different* object which we must try to decipher, at the cost of an effort which always risks failure. It is as if the quality enveloped, imprisoned the soul of an object other than the one it now designates. We "develop" this quality, this sensuous impression, like a tiny Japanese paper which opens under water and releases the captive form... Then, the sign's meaning appears, yielding to us the concealed object (Deleuze 1972: 11-12).

The existential imperative posed by a sensuous sign unfolds as a search in which the sign's affect is considered separately from the object it has been associated with. The affect of the sign is then taken into the 'development' of another object, which bears the same quality, only in a different association. It is not that the first object loses its sense; rather the sensuous sign is found in other objects simultaneously, such that it has multiple senses, acting as an affect common to multiple objects.

In this way, the sensuous sign is not "*abstract*", but "*general*" (Deleuze 2005: 278). It exists equally in all the bodies involved as a resemblance of quality, which forms an infinite order of objects bound by the same sensuous affect (Deleuze 1994: 1). This sign is never represented by a privileged instance, nor does it ever correspond with an abstract idea, rather objects intuitively follow from its quality, the mind perceiving more and more of them as it searches that quality. Thus, we must 'leap' towards every sensuous sign, actively seeking them in a movement of thought that takes the sign as the notion of infinite objects (Deleuze 2005: 283). The more we search it, the more we unfold the infinite power behind it, and thus experience the virtual realm of essential relation directly.

However, not all signs are sensuous or interpreted qualitatively. As we recall, signs participate in both the essence and existence of substance, which means that they face two realms. On the one hand, signs reflect the internal, invisible, and infinite essence of substance, which infinitely relates virtually (i.e. in infinite effects) so as to infinitely modify all attributes. On the other hand, the signs we perceive are merely modifications of thought that signify these effects and their particular essences in confused images. Consequently, between the essence and actuality of a sign there is an irreconcilable divide, and "Spinoza's analysis does not merely mark the irreducibility of these domains [but] proposes an explanation of signs which is a sort of genesis of [this] illusion" (Deleuze 2005: 58). Despite the fact that everything is in God/substance, and that it "is not, indeed, false to say that everything expresses God" (Deleuze 2005: 58),[56] or that substance's essence is the same as its existence (Spinoza 1992: 46-47), there nonetheless is a difference in kind between essence and its expression (49).[57] This difference is revealed by signs, which, in excess of their impression and appearance, stand out from other materials because they instantly relate themselves to a miscellany of other impressions. As though super-imposed upon the world, signs exude infinite meaning, their individual searches linking them to all impressions simultaneously. This simultaneous infinity of signs circulates out from them only to continually resonate back into them, as their affects finitely relate to each other and take on meaning. It is at this point that we erroneously believe that these ideas (i.e. affects of affects) actually represent their external truth (i.e. Ideas), as if the infinity of substance's essence could be finitely signified. Paradoxically, the search for truth engenders its own antithesis, producing images, ideas, and abstract understandings (i.e. ideas of ideas) that detract us from their true causes (i.e. effects).

---

[56] See also *Ethics*, II, 32 & proof (Spinoza 1992: 85).

[57] Substance's essence necessitates existence, being absolutely infinite and self-caused. However ,no mode of existence caused by substance is necessary. See *Ethics*, I, 24 & proof (Spinoza 1992: 49).

Signs and the Language
of Imagination

Using Spinoza's vocabulary, when the mind has an idea
of external bodies it is said to 'imagine':

> [T]o retain the usual terminology, we will assign the word
> 'images' (imagines) to those affections of the human body the
> ideas of which set forth external bodies as if they were present
> to us, although they do not represent shapes. And when the
> mind regards bodies in this way, we shall say that it 'imagines'
> (imaginari) (Spinoza 1992: 78).

As our essence meets another, the mind perceives an affect, an
amorphous sign that must be searched. Investigating this sign, it
begins to correlate to other affects, such that it is given definite
form and meaning relative to these. However, these 'ideas'
represent neither the actual 'shape' of the body affecting us nor
an actual quality of that body, but only an 'affect of its affect' on
us (82-85).

Whereby these affects of affects are 'images' that the
mind 'imagines', our 'imagination' is the "faculty of imagining"
various "contingent" ideas which represent external objects as if
they were part of our reality (78-79). In that all our ideas are
expressions of true Ideas/effects, these images must necessarily
follow from them and contain some truth, for:

> the imaginations of the mind, looked at in themselves, contain
> no error; i.e. the mind does not err from the fact that it
> imagines, but only in so far as it is considered to lack the [I]dea
> which excludes the existence of those things which it imagines
> to be present to itself (78).

This means that, "In so far as the human mind imagines
(*imaginatur*) an external body, to that extent is does not have an
adequate knowledge of it" (83). Imagining external bodies and
minds we deceive ourselves, for relative to our mind there is no
'other', no externality to our thoughts. Spinoza then

conceptualizes 'falsity' not as 'untruth', but as a type of confusion of the mind, a misrepresentation of essential relations, as the affect of one essence is used to signify that of another. Hence, the 'contingency' of images: whereby the Ideas causing them are infinite, our finite ideas cannot adequately represent them, despite the truth of their composite impressions (92-93). Thus, the imaginary is synonymous with what is inadequate in the mind: images, imaginary ideas (i.e. imaginations), and abstracts (i.e. 'ideas of ideas', or 'images of ideas').[58]

However, we must contrast the imaginary ideas and images of the mind with the act of imagining that conjures them. If images are associations of affects, and imaginary ideas are correlations of these, these significations come about because of invisible movements of thought, that associate and correlate them. The thinking mind, in contrast to the significant things that it thinks, receives the powers of substance, manifesting them as finite images in the attribute of thought.[59] Accordingly, the *act* of

---

[58] In his book on Hume, Deleuze has already analyzed imagination quite extensively, and found corroborative evidence for Spinoza's arguments. Like Spinoza before him, Hume discovered that the imagination is a passive faculty that receives ideas from external objects:

Nothing is done *by* the imagination; everything is done *in* the imagination. It is not even a faculty for forming ideas, because the production of an idea by the imagination is only the reproduction of an impression in the imagination. Certainly, the imagination has its own activity; but even this activity, being whimsical and delirious, is without constancy and without uniformity. It is the movement of ideas, and the totality of their actions and reactions. Being the place of ideas, the fancy is the collection of separate, individual items. Being the bond of ideas, it moves through the universe, engendering fire dragons, winged horses, and monstrous giants. The depth of the mind is indeed delirium, or – same thing from another point of view – change and indifference. By itself, the imagination is not nature; it is a mere fancy. There is no constancy or uniformity in the ideas that I have. No more is there constancy or uniformity in the way *in which ideas are connected through the imagination:* only chance makes up this connection (Deleuze 2001: 23).

As the imagination is affected by external bodies it is filled with impressions. Insofar as impressions represent each other to become images, the imagination does not produce images; rather the faculty of imagination is the repository of images produced by the effects of external bodies. As these external bodies relate, so do their images, their virtual association becoming a concrete association in the imagination. Consequently the imagination is filled with fanciful ideas and images, which are chaotically associated, in excess of their truth.

[59] See Deleuze's essay "The Image of Thought" (Deleuze 1994: 129-167).

imagining precedes all images, imaginations, and abstractions. This act of imagining is in all ways opposed to the faculty of imagination that it posits, which signifies signs. To search and think signs is instead 'to imagine' (*imaginator*), or the act of 'imagining', which assembles affects of the mind into finite 'images' (*imagos*), 'imaginary' (*imaginari*) and significant objects and relations, and other abstract 'imaginations' (*imaginatios*). Thus Deleuze can conclude from Spinoza that:

> The unity of all signs consists in this: they form an essentially equivocal language of imagination which stands in contrast to the natural language of philosophy, composed of univocal expressions. Thus, whenever a problem of signs is raised, Spinoza replies: such signs do not exist (*Treatise on the Intellect*, 36; *Ethics*, I, 10, schol. 1). It is characteristic of inadequate ideas to be signs that call for interpretations by the imagination, and not *expressions* amenable to *explications* by the lively intellect (concerning the opposition of explicative expressions and indicative signs, cf. II, 17, schol. And 18, schol.) (Deleuze 1988: 107).

Insofar as signs emerge amorphously and signify infinitely, they constitute a "language of imagination" wherein all affects are "equivocal". More like a 'proto-language', it constitutes forms without forming them into abstractions, linguistic or otherwise.[60] Like the participles of a language that never makes sense, searched signs and images remain polyvocal, freely associated such that they constitute a delirious state of forms-forming and images-imagined, where everything means everything. This 'language of imagination' is therefore synonymous with the act of imagining itself, in which essences are immediately received as the search of an array of infinite meanings.[61] This search ends when these infinite 'explications' get "fixed" in imaginary determinations, so that signs begin to correspond to specific

---

[60] This is a 'proto-language' and not a 'metalanguage' because the essence of this language still inheres within the impressions involved, and not outside them in a metaphysical realm.

[61] When Deleuze says "Learning is essentially concerned with *signs*" the sense of this is much clearer now: we learn through imagining/searching our signs (Deleuze 1972: 4).

images and ideas and take on particular meanings (Deleuze 2001: 23).

These imaginary determinations amount to a "language of philosophy" (or any other intellectual discipline for that matter), which proceeds according to significant and abstract linguistic expressions. These expressions are 'univocal' because their referents all have specific and redundant meanings, formed by the correlation of signs to affects in exclusive sets. These sets are then further signified by the various images and ideas of the mind, so that holistically they become a complete language in which 'intellect' proceeds. From this perspective, intelligence is an imaginary order, an infinite rhizome of codes (i.e. signifieds) and abstracts (i.e. ideas or images of ideas), wherein all signs must be 'interpreted' and given finite sense (i.e. significance) (Deleuze & Guattari 1987, 91).

Accordingly, making signs meaningful contradicts the equivocal nature of the sign itself. 'Meaningful signs' do not exist! Rather, signs become meaningful only after they stop 'signing', that is, after we stop searching them. If it is "characteristic" of inadequate ideas to become signs, it is because the signs that precede and posit them never stop signifying infinitely (Deleuze 1988: 107).

Now, as essences first appear before us as amorphous signs, our initial impressions and sensations must be closest to them, being their most immediate expressions, and reflecting their infinite potential to mean anything. Instead of comprehending these affects in terms of each other, if we could only sustain the initial state of sensing and imagining their impressions we would retain what is most truthful in them and hold the most adequate knowledge of their being. Ideally (i.e. relative to the Idea and essence of a sign, and not its significant ideas), we would perceive without images, and know without ideas.

Unfortunately, for what could only be called a 'lack of imagination',[62] we lapse again into the intellectual realm of the signified and the linguistic. Regretfully, these "Clear ideas give us nothing apart from some knowledge of a thing's properties,

---

[62] Or shall we say, a 'lack of imagining' so as to emphasize the activity and not its product, the verb and not the noun.

and lead us to nothing apart from a negative knowledge of its cause" (Deleuze 2005: 156). These 'clear ideas' are hardly clear at all, for in them the true Idea of an effect is exchanged for an image of affections, instead of a notion of their true effects. This creates a perpetual contradiction within our intellect, whereby all our intellectual and significant ideas are isolated from their truths in mere images of them. All our intelligent systems are therefore plagued with the fundamental error of attributing true causes to false images.

This is why Spinoza differentiates between " 'entities of imagination' (*entia imaginationis*)" and " 'entities of reason' (*entia rationis*)" in the *Ethics*. The former are "modes of imagining", which "denote not the nature of any thing but only the constitution of the imagination" (Spinoza 1992: 57-62).[63] We recognize at once that these entities of imagination are therefore significant images (i.e. imaginary ideas), as they represent a particular state of imagination with another (i.e. an affect of an affect; a mode of a mode). While 'reason', in the Spinozist sense, is reserved for the "the relations that enter into this composition, from which one deduces other relations (reasoning) and on the basis of which one experiences new feelings, active ones this time (feelings that *are born* of reason)" (Deleuze 1988: 56). Reason is an activity for Spinoza and Deleuze, the act of imagining (i.e. an active imagination; *imaginator*), or the expression of the new. It happens when signs correspond to their essential relations, for the essences are the only true 'reasons'. Thus, by searching signs we reason, as we are actively 'deducing' their infinite relations to all other essences and modes.[64]

Contrariwise, our various logical reflections, our various 'reasons' (i.e. concrete, finite, and passive; nouns) are contrary to "Reason" (i.e. virtual, infinite, and active essences/powers; the

---

[63] It is worth noting that Deleuze, in his first book, applied the exact same differentiation to Hume:

The contradiction, says Hume, is established between extension and reflection, imagination and reason, the senses and the understanding. In fact, this way of phrasing the issue is not the best, since it can apply to general rules as well. Elsewhere, Hume says it more clearly: the contradiction is established between the *principles of the imagination and the principles of reason* (Deleuze 2001: 81-82).

[64] Instead of making significant abductions of their external causes.

verb; the singular act of reasoning, which Deleuze designates with a capital 'R') (55), and the alliance of our imagination with the essences of substance.[65] Truth, therefore, flourishes above the imaginary principles of the intellect when we restore all our ideas to their composite impressions and search them as if they were infinitely meaningful. Decomposing our ideas in this manner, "the ideas we have [become] signs, indicative images impressed in us, rather than expressive ideas formed by us: [the act of] perception or imagination, rather than comprehension" (Deleuze 2005: 147). In this way, signs unite with their essences so as to continue to propel thought, relegating the mind to the chaos of the infinite act of imagining, instead of the finiteness of an intelligence already imagined. Passive, habitual, and memorial expressions must everywhere be opposed to the acts of imagining, sensing, and thinking that precede them, which manifest the essences, powers, and truths of life (Deleuze 1988: 74).

The Imagination Program

In his study on Proust, Deleuze gives us a sense of what a 'language of imagination' would look like, and how it is manifested in the real. Adding to Spinoza's arguments, he observes that the infinite signs and notions that lead us to truth are found most predominantly among concrete 'works of art'. This is because the concrete work of art is characterized not only by its ability to affect us, but by its ability to affects us differently every time we encounter it. In this way, the work of art insinuates invisible essences that relate to our own, the effects and Ideas of said relations affecting our body and mind respectively (Deleuze 1972: 39-50). Art not only "reveals the transitory as absolute" (De Beauvoir: 80), but manifests "absolute and ultimate Difference" (Deleuze 1972: 41), the infinite 'Difference' (note Deleuze's capitalization of the word)

---

[65] The term 'logical reflections' is a tautology: all reflections are logical, for insofar as they are meaningful they belong a logic of intelligence, of affects exclusively correlated to affects.

of substance, the essence of which differentiates new affections from those already differentiated.[66]

No matter how we engage art, in thought or in act, it possesses us and leads us towards a cornucopia of creative activities. As we become physically and mentally involved with the work, our body and mind mix with its materials such that its essence is constituted through our artistic effort to interpret and respond to the work's signs. These signs of art:

> give us the true unity: unity of an immaterial sign and of an entirely spiritual meaning. The essence is precisely this unity of sign and meaning as it is revealed in the work of art. Essences or Ideas, that is what each sign of the [work of art] reveals (40-41).

If "essence is always an artistic essence", it is because every essential relation is expressed as new affects, which we then artificially interpret with imaginary ideas of external causes (50).

In the presence of a work of art, we are overwhelmed by signs, for as our essence meets that of the work of art we experience completely new impressions, the novelty of which forces us to search them. However, we search them in and through that which is closest to them, namely the work of art, such that these signs keep coming back to these effects, re-affecting us and re-producing signs within us. Art becomes a perpetual search, a series of signs that lead only to signs, or truths that lead only to others. It "*is the work of art which produces within itself and upon itself its own effects, and is filled with them, and nourished by them:* the work of art is nourished by the truths it engenders" (136). Art engenders truth because it allows for the continual interaction of essences, compounding their effects and subsequent affects:

> Art therefore has an absolute privilege, which is expressed in several ways. In art, substances are spiritualized, media

---

[66] Essential "differen*t*iation" virtually differentiates new affects that differ from each other according to concrete and finite "differen*c*iations", which are images of the former (Deleuze 1994: 206-208).

> dematerialized. The work of art is therefore a world of signs,
> but they are immaterial and no longer have anything opaque
> about them: at least to the artist's eye, the artist's ear. In the
> second place, the meaning of these signs is an essence, an
> essence affirmed in all its power. In the third place, sign and
> meaning, essence and transmuted substance are identified or
> united in a perfect adequation. Identity of a sign, as style, and
> of a meaning as essence: such is the character of the work of
> art (49).

As if 'dematerialized' or 'spiritualized' these materials signify
infinitely, instead of particularly. Hence their transparency: they
can mean anything. Staying signs, they remain true to their
effects and essences, expressing differences from within the
already different materials of the work of art, and unifying the
work of art in an autogenesis of impressions.

Works of art consequently function like 'machines', as
these virtual relations are mimicked in concrete ones:

> The modern work of art is anything it may seem; it is even its
> very property of being whatever we like, of having the
> overdetermination of whatever we like, from the moment *it
> works*: the modern work of art is a machine an functions such...
> [The work of art is] machine and machinery whose meaning
> (anything you like) depends solely on its functioning, which, in
> turn, depends on its separate parts. The modern work of art has
> no problem of meaning, it has only a problem of use.
>
> Why a machine? Because the work of art, so
> understood, is essentially productive- productive of certain
> truths. No one has insisted more than Proust on the following
> point: that the truth is produced, that it is produced by orders of
> machines which function within us, that it is extracted from our
> impressions, hewn out of our life, delivered in a work (128-9).

The work of art literally 'works', turning out different affects and
affections every time we use it. Although composed of common
qualities and stable materials, the meaning of the work of art is
only determined by the situation in which it is used. We may
recognize a particular "style" or 'theme' in a work of art, but

when we try to actually understand it we always come up with different answers, for as the stock of our impressions constantly shifts, the work of art takes on different meanings.[67] Art 'works' precisely because it rearranges our impressions, its power to do so coming from the essential relations inhering within it. And this is how we recognize art as art: it never fails to produce new meaning and significance, which is to say that it never stops *working*.[68] Free from necessary object or meaning, the work of art unites disparate elements and worlds together in a play of images and understandings, warping our preconceived notions and systems of understanding. We sustain its effect by holding fast to the signs of art, searching them deeply so that they can have their way with our perception and imagination.

The machine of art, therefore, creates a perpetual rift between the world of the concrete and the powers of the virtual within it. Art cuts the concrete with the virtual. As we engage art, our imagination goes wild with impressions, ideas, and images, as its essence relates to our own, modifying our body and mind infinitely. Searching and following art, or creating a work of art ourselves, we make real the very essences of signs, and disclose the truth of substance's powers. Thus, if we are genuinely looking for the truth, we are best to start with art for all works of art represent concentrations of those universal signs that manifest the essences of substance and produce their infinite reality.

When Deleuze argues that the imagination is the repository of truth, he implicitly argues that those searching for truth should become artists, for nothing activates the imagination more than observing art and endeavoring to create it. In fact, the

---

[67] Styles vary not only between works of art, but between individuals, for every person has their own essence, just like every work of art. As essences vary from person to person, everyone is affected differently by a work of art, for we each bring a different body and mind to it (Deleuze 1972: 39-50). Common sense has already informed us of this fact, art being well popularized as a 'subjective' experience, affecting each of us in our own way, despite the commonality of the work's materials and forms.

[68] A true work of art is recognizable by its uncanny ability to continually re-compose our ideas, emotions, and other reactions. And this makes sense, for we come to the work of art each time as a different person, a different body. Our essence may be constant, but our body is affected by others, and thus its materials continually change relative to those.

act of imagining *is* art insofar as it represents the threshold at which essence is expressed in the concrete and the concrete returns to its essences. And art is essential for that very reason: art is the production of the artificial, the manufacture of modes, the very power of substance to express itself. Extending Deleuze's Spinozism, we can conclude from these observations that the true act is an infinite act of art, just as true thought is the infinite act of imagining.

Throughout this process, the artistic endeavour stands in contrast to the intellectual pursuit. Although the work of art may contain and produce images, ideas, and abstracts, the work itself cannot be contained by anyone of them. Whatever finite relations it calls into play are reproduced through an artistic essence that scrambles all their codes and rearranges them into new affects. Art does so because its signs enjoy the 'privilege' of two ontological realms, being part essential relation, and part modality at the same time. In the search of art, essence transubstantiates itself, becoming infinitely affective and meaningful. Art gives us a privileged view of infinity thrust upon us from without, illuminating and spiritualizing matter, stripping it of all limits and boundaries, and circulating it in all worlds and understandings simultaneously, like a semiotic ghost passing through walls.

The signs of art break the illusion of a finite truth, which is the fundamental illusion of human existence in which we are deceived and misled by our intelligence towards thinking and feeling as if we have grasped what our senses and affections truly allude to, namely infinite essential relations. Ironically, our most abstract ideas, our most rarefied understandings, are actually symbols of an incredible repression of the truth, for in each one the truth of an affect is buried in another mode. Against this repression, against these finite images and ideas that never reach their infinite essences, Spinoza and Deleuze are tacitly arguing for something that is more like a pure experience of truth, a direct intuition of substance's power.

At its limit, Spinozism approaches a Taoist or Zen-like state wherein "we go beyond Reason as a faculty of the common notions or a system of eternal truths concerning existence and enter into the *intuitive intellect* as a system of essential truths"

(Deleuze 1988: 58).[69] In contrast to a life contemplated and analyzed, Spinozism offers us a life lived in communion with the infinite essences of substance. It is an intuitive way of living, filled with fleeting movements and impressions that flow without preconception. We sustain it so long as we sustain our search of signs and their affects, considering them universally, abstracting from abstraction itself and re-positing our search in the process of infinite abstraction, or the same, the relentless search for new meaning.

Consequently, substance's powers are maximized as essences are allowed to work symbiotically together, rather than suppressing each other in abstract images. From this perspective, Deleuze's Spinoza is beginning to sound much more like Nietzsche, espousing a will to power of substance, with a drive towards the greatest degree of power, the greatest degree of truth.[70] His natural language of imagination is a natural language of power, with essences and truths infinitely related and infinitely compounded. Spinozism here gives way to a language of signs that revolves around works of art, their true effects and the infinite production of new affects. Signs lead us to an art of life, a living art of making true essences real so that we can surpass illusions of meaning in favour of intuitive creation.[71]

---

[69] "The sage waits for the event, that is to say, *understands the pure event* in its truth, independently of its spatio-temporal actualization, as something eternally yet to come and always already passed... But at the same time, the sage also *wills the embodiment* and the actualization of the pure incorporeal event in a state of affairs and in his or her own body and flesh" (Deleuze 1990 *Negotiations*: 136-7, 146). The pure event is always an essence, whose truth is beyond significant understanding, instead embodied in an act.

[70] The comparison was not lost on Deleuze, who begins *Spinoza: Practical Philosophy* with an homage to Nietzsche and to everything Nietzschean about Spinoza's works (Deleuze 1988: 3).

[71] And yet Badiou audaciously calls Spinozism a "philosophy of death", claiming that "death is, above all else, that which is *simultaneously* most intimately related to the individual it affects in a relationship of absolute impersonality or exteriority to this individual. In this sense, it *is* thought, for thinking consists precisely in ascetically attaining that point where the individual is transfixed by the impersonal exteriority that is equally his or her own authentic being" (Badiou 2000: 12). In this passage, Badiou seems to ignore the fact that for Deleuze (as for his mentor, Bergson) thought is the very antithesis of death, and the truth of life. Life is characterized by the absence of individuality, by a mind which "change[s] without ceasing" (Bergson 2005: 2). The significant stratum in which individuality is inscribed therefore has "no reality" (3), or as Deleuze would say,

Spinoza the artist, Spinoza the semiotician — this is how Deleuze interprets his teacher, with the *Ethics* and the *Treatise* being the greatest examples of his work of art, genuine handbooks for the infinite production of the living real.

---

no 'truth'. "[A]n ego which does not change does not *endure*" (3), rather what is living in us is the persistence of "*lived*" experience in spite of whatever "abstract" individuality we may ascribe to ourselves or the universe (7). Therefore the exteriority of intellect is not death, but is at most a "partial death", as the mind turns from the significant strata of our 'subjectivity', towards the essential, where "neither [significant] bodies nor speaking persons" exist (Deleuze 2000: 121). In this way, what is living in us is never individual or subjective, but is more like a "zone of subjectivation" in which individual forms get are perpetually broken apart and reassembled (120-124).

Secondly, Badiou seems to have also ignored Deleuze's Spinozist arguments about death. Quite simply put, in Spinozism there is no death, as all essences are absolutely eternal. At the level of modes though, affects and affections continually pass in and out of concrete existence, which creates an image of death. As modes end their "duration", we fallaciously imagine that the essences causing them to expire with them (Deleuze 1988: 62-63).

Works Cited

Badiou, Alain. (2000) *Deleuze: The Clamor of Being*. Minneapolis: Minnesota Press.

Bergson, Henri. (1991) *Matter and Memory*. New York: Zone Books.

Bergson, Henri (2005) *Creative Evolution*. New York: Barnes & Nobel.

Casey, Timothy & Embree, Lester, eds. (1990) *Lifeworld and Technology*. Lanham: University Press of America.

De Beauvoir (1976) *The Ethics of Ambiguity*. New York: Citadel Press.

Delanda, Manuel. (2002) *Intensive Science and Virtual Philosophy*. New York: Continuum Books.

Deleuze, Gilles. (1991), *Bergsonism*. New York: Zone Books.

--- (2004), *Desert Islands and Other Texts: 1953-1974*. New York: Semiotext(e).

--- (1994), *Difference and Repetition*. New York: Columbia University Press.

--- (2001), *Empiricism and Subjectivity: An Essay on Hume's Theory of Human Nature*. New York: Columbia University Press.

--- (1997), *Essays Critical and Clinical*. Minneapolis: University of Minnesota Press.

--- (2005), *Expressionism in Philosophy: Spinoza*. Brooklyn: Zone Books.

--- (2000), *Foucault*. Minneapolis: University of Minnesota Press.

--- (1990), *Logic of Sense*. New York: Columbia University Press.

--- (1990), *Negotiations*. New York: Columbia University Press.

---(1972) *Proust and Signs*. Minneapolis: University of Minnesota Press.

--- (1988), *Spinoza: Practical Philosophy*. San Francisco: City Lights Books.

Deleuze, Gilles and Guattari, Félix. (1987), *A Thousand Plateaus*. Minneapolis: University of Minnesota Press.

Deleuze, Gilles and Parnet, Claire. (1987), *Dialogues*. New York: Columbia University Press.

Heidegger, Martin. (1972), *What is Called Thinking?* New York: Harper Torchbooks.

Hume, David. (1961), *A Treatise of Human Nature: Volume I*. New York: J. M. Dent & Sons Ltd.

James, William. (1974), *Pragmatism: and Four Essays from The Meaning of Truth*. New York: New American Library.

Nietzsche, Friedrich. (1969), *Thus Spoke Zarathustra*. New York: Penguin Books.

Leibniz, G. W. (1991), *Discourse on Metaphysics and Other Essays*. Indianapolis: Hackett Publishing.

Marcel, Gabriel. (2002), *The Philosophy of Existentialism*. New York: Citadel Press.

Mauss, Marcel. (1990), *The Gift*. New York: W.W. Norton.

Plato. (1945), *The Republic*. New York: Oxford University Press.

Plotinus. (1992), *The Enneads*. New York: Larson Publications.

Proust, Marcel. (1998-2003), *In Search of Lost Time, Vols. I-VI*. New York: Modern Library.

Rand, Ann. (1990), *Introduction to Objectivist Epistemology*. Toronto: Signet.

Saussure, Ferdinand de. (2005), *Course in General Linguistics*. Chicago: Open Court.

Sartre, Jean-Paul. (1994), *Being and Nothingness*. Toronto: Random House.

Sebeok, Thomas. (2001), *Signs: An Introduction to Semiotics*. Toronto: University of Toronto Press.

Schirmacher, Wolfgang. (1984), *Social Science Information 23, 3*.

Spinoza, Baruch. (1992), *Ethics; Treatise on the Emendation of the Intellect; Selected Letters*. Indianapolis: Hackett Publishing Company.

Stubenberg, Leopold. (2005), "Neutral Monism", in *Stanford Encyclopedia of Philosophy*. Stanford University, 2007. <http://plato.stanford.edu/entries/neutral-monism/>

Wittgenstein, Ludwig. *The Blue and Brown Books*. (1960), Toronto: Harper Torchbooks.

Žižeck, Slavoj. (2004), *Organs Without Bodies*. New York: Routledge.

Think Media: EGS Media Philosophy Series

Wolfgang Schirmacher, editor

The Ethics of Uncertainty: Aporetic Openings. Michael Anker

Trans/actions: Art, Film and Death. Bruce Alistair Barber

Trauma, Hysteria, Philosophy. Hannes Charen and Sarah Kamens

Literature as Pure Mediality: Kafka and the Scene of Writing.
Paul DeNicola

Deleuze and the Sign. Christopher M. Drohan

Imaginality: Conversant and Eschaton. A. Staley Groves

Hospitality in the age of media representation. by Christian Hänggi

**The Organic Organisation: freedom, creativity and
the search for fulfilment.** Nicholas Ind

Media Courage: impossible pedagogy in an artificial community.
Fred Isseks

Mirrors triptych technology: Remediation and Translation Figures.
Diana Silberman Keller

Sonic Soma: Sound, Body and the Origins of the Alphabet.
Elise Kermani

**The Art of the Transpersonal Self: Transformation as Aesthetic and Energetic
Practice.** Norbert Koppensteiner

Can Computers Create Art? James Morris

Propaganda of the Dead: Terrorism and Revolution. Mark Reilly.

The Novel Imagery: Aesthetic Response as Feral Laboratory. Dawan Stanford.

Community without Identity: The Ontology and Politics of Heidegger.
Tony See

other books available from Atropos Press

Teletheory. Gregory L. Ulmer

Philosophy of Culture-Kulturphilosophie: Schopenhauer and Tradition. Edited by
Wolfgang Schirmacher.

Virilio: Grey Ecology. The La Rochelle Workshop.
Edited by Hubertus von Amelunxen. Translated by Drew Burk

Talking Cheddo: Liberating PanAfrikanism. Menkowra Manga Clem Marshall

The Tupperware Blitzkrieg. Anthony Metivier

Che Guevara and the Economic Debate in Cuba. Luiz Bernardo Pericás

Follow Us or Die. Vincent W.J. van Gerven Oei and Jonas Staal

Just Living: Philosophy in Artificial Life. Collected Works Volume 1.
Wolfgang Schirmacher